Acting

While all value judgements about the arts are problematical, there does seem to be a special problem with acting. Everyone seems to be able to act. It seems to be the easiest of arts; if an art at all. Moreover, the better the technique, the easier it seems. This book examines how we think of acting, the language we use, and the criteria we employ to distinguish good acting from bad.

It addresses itself to the intellectual problems associated with the idea of acting, for example, how we distinguish the actor from the character. It covers the range of contemporary actor training and practice from Stanislavski to the post-modern, and examines the spiritual and moral purpose of acting within society: why we need to act.

Acting integrates professional experience with intellectual enquiry. While not a 'how to' book, it is a broad enquiry into how and why it is done. Rooted in performance needs, it will be of interest to all intelligent theatre-goers, as well as actors and students of theatre.

John Harrop has over thirty years' experience of the professional theatre, as both actor and director. He has taught acting and directing to professional drama students in the United Kingdom, North America and Australia, and is co-author of *Creative Play Direction*, and *Acting with Style*.

Theatre Concepts
Edited by John Russell Brown
Michigan University

Theatre Concepts is a new series designed to encourage a precise understanding of each aspect of theatre practice. Most books on the theatre promote a particular personal or theoretical point of view. Theatre Concepts are written by experienced practitioners in direct and accessible language in order to open up debates and experience of theatre.

Acting

John Harrop

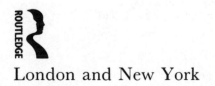

London and New York

First published 1992
by Routledge
11 New Fetter Lane, London EC4P 4EE

Simultaneously published in the USA and Canada
by Routledge
a division of Routledge, Chapman and Hall Inc.
29 West 35th Street, New York, NY 10001

Phototypeset in 10 on 12 point Baskerville by
Intype, London
Printed in Great Britain by
Clays Ltd, St Ives plc

British Library Cataloguing in Publication Data
Harrop, John
  Acting. – (Theatre concepts series)
  I. Title II. Series
792.028

Library of Congress Cataloging in Publication Data
Harrop, John
    Acting / John Harrop.
      p.   cm. — (Theatre concepts series)
    Includes bibliographical references and index.
    1. Acting. 2. Acting—Study and teaching. I. Title.
II. Series.
PN2061.H328   1992
792'.028—dc20   91–40570

ISBN 0–415–05961–5   ISBN 0–415–05962–3 (pbk)

Contents

Acknowledgements

I should like to thank all the actors I have ever worked with or taught; Tom Markus and Sabin Epstein for counsel and caring; my sometime colleague Oliver Gerland for chats about contemporary criticism; above all, the General Editor of this series, John Russell Brown, without whose encouragement and kindly perceptive advice this book would not have been written.

Introduction

As the classical tag tells us: *de gustibus non est disputandum*. All aesthetic judgements will be problematical. But there does seem to be a special problem with acting. Is it an art at all; or merely a craft? If it is an art, it seems to be the easiest, the cheapest of arts, perhaps akin to photography where anyone can do it, even with a box-brownie. Schnozzle Durante told us many years ago that 'Everybody wants to get into the act.' A highly prescient remark in that, since the advent of television, programmes featuring 'Real People' have topped the ratings – at least in the US. Everybody seems able to act. Indeed, current sociopsychological sensibility propounds the idea that we are all acting all the time in everyday life. What then is particular about 'acting' in theatrical terms? The classic layperson's response to acting is: 'How did you learn all those lines?' The other response most actors get if they divulge their profession is: 'Oh yes. I was in a play in the third grade.' And, of course, they were. But violinists tend not to get the response 'Oh yes. I played the violin in the third grade', nor artists, 'I did finger painting in nursery school.'

Acting seems easy and, irony of ironies, the better the technique, the easier it seems. The problem of discussing what it means to be the 'abstracts and chronicles of our time', has defied the best attempts of philosophers, critics and especially those practitioners, who, in a somewhat diffident and surprised manner, have tried to write about what it is they do! Alec Guinness has stated the conundrum: 'I am not at all sure what great acting is and yet, when seen, it is instantly recognizable.'[1] So, it will be the attempt of this book, at the risk of making 'the unskilful laugh . . . [and] the judicious grieve',[2] to uncover what it is that is 'instantly recognizable'. To examine how we may think and speak about acting. What, if it is possible to make judgements, are the criteria; and what language can or should we use in discourse?

The approach will be to look at the actor as sign and sacrifice, both in the context of what constitutes his or her versatility, and in the context of the needs of the various theatrical constituencies – audience, critic, director, instructor – to communicate with one another in discussing acting.

There seem to be two basic reasons for the problematic nature of this discussion. The actor is at the same time the artist and the instrument: 'How can we know the dancer from the dance?' as Yeats has asked in a related context.[3] This problem has been compounded, since the advent of naturalism in the theatre, by the idea that it is the aim of acting to disguise its own artifice; that virtuosity's function is to eliminate any display of virtuosity; that to appear 'real' or 'normal' is the criterion of excellence.

One of the basic problems for the actor is not to let thinking get in the way of doing. It is equally a problem for appraising acting. The form of the discussion can alter the nature of the discussed. Such language and criteria as have been used in the past to discuss acting have been literary. This is not unreasonable. Performance tends to be based upon a script, which at least appears to be concrete and to stand still while it is being judged. Now acting conspicuously does not do this, unless it is captured on film and held in a still frame to be looked at; at which time it seems to invite the criteria of photography or pictorial art. Even the seemingly concrete part of talking about acting, the technical how-to-do-it, fails to come to grips with substance. Of the hundreds of acting manuals written since Stanislavski's first attempt to analyse the art scientifically, maybe six have anything more to offer than the classic: 'One of the musts for the actor of straight parts is an upright posture.' No pun intended by the author.

It may well be impossible to talk about acting as if it were a single 'thing'. Is there some 'thing' present in the performance of Shakespeare, Nōh, Kathakali, Brecht? Is it a change in form or merely a question of adjustment of style? Are instincts and talent universal qualities? Can we even suggest that in a period of critical deconstruction? Could Thespis talk to Burbage, Tarleton, Duse, Garrick, Talma, Irving, Bernhardt, Brando and Olivier? What kind of language would they use? Or would they all just smile and nod to each other in a secret, conspiratorial way?

It is certainly not the intention of this book to try to produce an ANSWER. The attempt will be to identify the problems, to examine them in the various areas of the acting experience, to discover how far it is possible to speak of salient or common features, and to provide fuel and a structure for thought and discussion. With Alec Guinness we all seem to intuit that at the bottom we recognize good acting when we see it. What this book will try to do is to examine how far that intuition can have a basis in denominators that allow common ways of thinking and shared means of discussion.

The arc of the discussion will range from intellectual issues associated with the idea of acting – the phenomenological problem, and the attempt of semiotics to provide an objective language for appraisal – through the technical means by which an actor brings acting about; to what might be called acting as a ritual testing of the soul. Precisely because, as has been suggested, surface criteria seem so glib, it is the more important that some attempt should be made to examine these criteria in all the problematical dimensions of the actor's art. In this way when, if not judgement, but at least serious discussion does take place, some however uncertain common understanding may be available.

And, while pursuing this necessarily academic process, the book will try not to forget that, at a very basic level, acting is putting on funny walks and making funny faces. As Laurence Olivier is reported to have said to Dustin Hoffman, who was preparing for *Marathon Man* by an exceedingly hard routine of runs and exercises, 'I pretend, dear boy, I pretend.' Or as a friend of mine once said to me when I was explaining the deep moral, social and political significance of Kenneth Tynan's *Oh, Calcutta!* 'Oh, come on John! It's just a good old bum and tit show, got up *pour épater les bourgeois!'*

Chapter 1

Acting and the phenomenological problem

Discussion of the acting process usually resolves itself into the received dichotomy of emotion versus technique. This dialogue goes back at least as far as Diderot, who gave it a first complete examination in his *Le Paradoxe sur le comédien* (1830).[1] Most recently it has been illustrated by the conflict, dear to the journalists of the 1940s and 1950s, between 'feelers' and 'nonfeelers'; adherents, mostly Americans, of the 'Method', and those, said to be British, who supposedly based their technique on physical and verbal skills alone.

The debate derives its force from the phenomenological fact that an actor has, in a sense, to be both himself and someone else at the same time. This kind of paradox is dear to the academic mind and, while it has more truth in philosophy than praxis – unlike philosophers and literary critics, actors are obliged to make a specific choice in the moment of action – yet in the realm of language it is a problem. And it is in language that we are obliged to discuss the nature of acting. Clearly, we do not find it impossible to talk about a play: we say that such and such a performance was good or bad; such and such a design worked or didn't. But what are our criteria for judgement? Is there such a thing as acting *per se* – the *Ding an sich*? Can it, in the theatre, ever be divorced from characterization, for example? Do we not always see the actor as a character? We acknowledge this at the end of the performance; we applaud the actors for their skill and art in playing the characters. We are especially aware of this skill if we happen to know the play, if the role is a famous one, if we have our own conception of it. Here we will tend to have not just a paradox but a triple image: we see an actor playing a character which is in apposition to a concept in our mind.

If we compare the experience of theatre-going with being present at any other form of art performance or entertainment, the problem with acting becomes clearer. At the simplest level, the muscle-man, the Miss Universe contestant and the stand-up comedian are projecting themselves. They may be making adaptations to the conventions of the performance, but they are not playing a charac-ter. Likewise the artist, the musician, even the dancer, either creates an artefact separate from him- or herself, or is the subject of the performance. Only the actor is both present on stage and yet at the same time absent, replaced by the illusion he or she creates. If the actor 'appears', it is usually through a break in the illusion – a stumble, the forgetting of a line, a missed entrance – which only serves to remind us of the duality. The adoption of otherness while remaining oneself is an essential and highly dynamic attribute of the actor's art.

In one sense, of course, actors are storytellers; and if they were simply storytellers, as Homer of old and his many descendants down through the Middle Ages to our stand-up comedians today (it is a sad comment upon our world that our storytellers today no longer tell heroic tales but only jokes), then they would be speaking in their own person. But the combination of storytelling and mimetic ritual that created our theatre has complicated our ability to talk about it, in bringing us the modern actor who takes on, in more than one sense, the character that stands against his or her name in the programme. When this actor says 'I' he means 'I, Hamlet' or 'I, Blanche Du Bois', not 'I, myself'. The ancient storyteller began, '*Arma virumque cano*', (I sing of arms and the man). When Bernard Shaw sang of *Arms and the Man* it was not his voice we heard (though Shaw may be an unfortunate choice here in that it was always his voice we heard), but the voices of Bluntschli, Saranoff, etc. The whole conundrum was put upon the stage itself by Luigi Pirandello, specifically in his *Six Characters in Search of an Author* (1921).[2] Pirandello's stage metaphor set out the limitations of acting as a means of expressing reality through the layering device of having actors playing 'real' people who were trying to establish their reality by having actors perform their lives for them on stage.

Despite the fact that the actor means 'I the character', not 'I myself' when he or she speaks on stage, in one inevitable sense it is the 'I myself' that the audience sees. No matter how actors act, they cannot expunge themselves from the performance or there will be no performance there. And this 'I-ness' is a necessary part of the theatre. It gives actors a good part of their interest, their specialness. They are performing; they are the *sine qua non* of the occasion; they are there, even when most pretending not to be. The playwright's intention only comes into being through them.

This is fine and splendidly true in the realm of rhetoric, but it does not help us to be specific about what acting is. More than that, the mention of the playwright brings up the whole problem of the other elements that go toward realizing a character upon the stage: costumers, set designers, directors, all can contribute to making the actor in character seem good or bad. Can we, then, ever focus simply on the 'acting'? How do we say the character was badly written but well acted; the actor did well despite being badly directed?

Are there aspects of acting that can be singled out as such, elements which will, of course, be present in what the actor creates on stage, but may be viewed separately from the illusion of character? I think there may be. We will still, perhaps, disagree about their level of excellence – after all, not everyone cares for a Van Gogh or Picasso, even at 40 million dollars a shot – but just as we can say a football player played well though his side was badly beaten, so we can with an actor identify a similar range of factors which are better or worse in his or her work. The analogy holds even better with tennis players. The Australian Yvonne Gulagong did not win nearly as many games or championships as Chris Evert, but I, and many others, preferred to watch her play. It was grace versus efficiency, erratic brilliance versus great competence: Gulagong could not hit the ball out of court and lose the point without making a perfectly balanced graceful shot.

This potentially raises a further problem: not only must we distinguish the actor from the character, but we must be able to say how well the actor performed as actor, rather than in character terms. At the very least, we can probably define the elements we must look at. After all the playwright writes for an instrument – just as Mozart wrote for the Stradivarius – the actor's body, voice, legs, arms, torso, hair, hands, feet, etc. These have their own physical vocabulary of potentiality. The way in which they are used will of course differ in different times and according to the demands of different styles; but the instrument hasn't changed, and we can look at the technical vocabulary, and examine the sliding scale of values and techniques along which acting is practised.

To do this will probably help us to establish how the good actor goes about his or her business. It may not be as useful with great acting. How do you examine the kiss of the gods? We may admire the imprint, but the substance is harder to define. And however we render down the illusion, whatever practical perspective we take, the phenomenological problem of acting will always be with us; the actor is both himself and the character at the same time.

We can see how the Greek term for actor (*hypokrites*) came to assume the modern sense of the word 'hypocrite': the actor does not answer for him- or herself. He or she answers with someone else's words. Actors also allow themselves to be used, both by the playwright and the audience, and the association here between actor and prostitute becomes apparent. Of course, there is also the more positive sense of this giving, which we shall discuss later: the actors' ritual sacrifice of their bodies for the good of society.

By whatever standard and in whatever perspective, the duality or duplicity of the actor on stage is a fundamental element of theatre. The actor is a real person living in an unreal way. Which reality do we judge? Perhaps the most famous example of the ironical infusion, or confusion of nature with art was Molière, taking ill – and later dying – while playing *Le Malade imaginaire* on stage.

While coming to terms with this dilemma, our purpose is not to try to examine it away. It is precisely part of the fascination of the actor that he or she does artificially what everyone else does naturally, and tries to make the artifice natural. Then, if it is too natural, how can we know what the actor is doing to achieve the art that disguises art: the imitation of an action, in Aristotle's sense, and an action in itself – calculated yet meant to appear effortless.

Corresponding to the duality of emotion and technique, mentioned at the beginning of this section, there tend to be two basic modes of acting, which brings up the further issue of the possible need for more than one set of criteria. These modes may be termed self-expressive[3] and self-effacing. The first mode is virtuoso whereby the actor tends to devour the part, substituting him- or herself for the character. The 'grand' classical roles lend themselves to this mode; they are there to be conquered and actors take them on to prove they are up to it. The audience will always be aware of the actor in the role, and they tend to become associated with the part: Olivier's *Othello*, Gielgud's *Hamlet*, Wolfit's *King Lear* and, to show that this can happen in supposedly 'naturalistic' roles, Brando's Kowalski. This mode of acting may be compared with other art forms such as opera, dance, Marceau's mime, where it tends to be about what is displayed and who displays it, rather than the co-operative effect of the story. Sometimes great actors deliberately reveal their virtuosity in this mode with pieces of personal business that are remembered after the rest of the performance has paled. In another context of playing, this would happen with the great English soccer player Stanley Matthews, who would sometimes beat his man twice to the delight of the crowd, just to show that he could do it.

In this mode we are always very much aware of the actor in the part. Arthur Symonds has said of Sarah Bernhardt that she is 'always the actress as well as the part'. At her best she balanced the two 'I's' and the audience's consciousness of one did not disturb the balance of the other. At less than her best, the audience would still see the 'incomparable craftswoman labouring at her work'.

The other mode is more usually associated with the 'realistic' approach, Duse quietly hiding herself within the character, 'forcing her soul' to its 'conceit'. Or the work of Alec Guinness comes to mind; the total subsuming of self into character. A skill which often earns the title of 'actor's actor', a virtuosity which may only be fully recognized by other professionals, for it tends to lack the magic of alchemy in its photographic reproduction of detail. This mode may well be responsible for the imposition of the false criterion of truth to external detail, upon the art of acting.

Criteria of 'good acting' have tended to become unbalanced toward the self-effacing mode since audience address was left behind in the eighteenth century. Melodrama did in fact keep that tradition going into the late nineteenth century, but, regarded as a debased form, it did not provide a model by which acting might be judged. Since theatre sealed off the audience in front of the fourth wall, the actor has more and more effaced him- or herself within the character. This may have tended to disguise the phenomenological problem in discussing the actor's art, but it doesn't negate it.

The very last ceremony of the play, the curtain call, is there to remind us of the phenomenological, not to say ontological, issue. The dead rise from the stage and the actors return to us in their own persons, smiling out behind the motley to acknowledge our applause of their virtuosity. Something supernatural has been taking place, and the weary humility (another mask) with which the actor seeks to reveal and dispel his or her part in it, makes it even harder for us to reconcile this very human one of us with the character we have just seen. All may be revealed, but the necessary hypocrisies both audience and actor accept – the actor keeps up the illusion that the audience doesn't exist, the audience suspends its disbelief that the actor does – make it hard to find a true basis for what has taken place. What was actor, what was character? In order to clear up the problem, and turn everything on stage into an objective vocabulary of signs which might be understood and shared by all the theatrical constituencies, semiotics was born.

Chapter 2

Acting and semiotics

In the twentieth century, critical attempts to deal with the nature of theatre have been catching up with acting practice. The movement has been away from discussion of the play as literary artefact to the effect which the performance of that artefact makes on the stage. In this process the not unsurprising discovery has been made that it is in action, not just language, that theatre communicates with its audience. Actors have always known this, and Aristotle dropped fairly strong hints some time ago. Theorists accepted this concept, but have been unable to act upon it owing to the attempt to discuss action in terms of a literary form. The discovery that a language of performance is necessary to discuss performance, puts critics somewhat in the position of Molière's Monsieur Jourdain who discovered late in life that he had been speaking prose all his life without having been aware of it.

In the theatre, words are heard not read, and movement is seen. The Elizabethan theatre, one of the most dynamic in theatrical history, itself flourished in an age when the majority of people were illiterate. What impresses the audience is gestures, movements, sounds and images. These become, in the language of semiotics, the 'signs' that theatre sends out and which the audience recognizes. In this context, the subjective actors become an objective sign when seen within the frame of the theatrical event. All the visible and aural elements of the stage contribute to the total meaning: vocal inflexions, set, costume, makeup, the actor's body. The audience is bombarded by visual images from the stage in a manner which, however much the words may jump off the page, it is not when in the study. Indeed, in a fundamental way, what a director tries to do is to integrate all this input in the audience's consciousness – to 'frame the action', to borrow a cinematic term – in such a way that a particular meaning will be conveyed at a particular moment; and the incremental meaning of all the particular moments will be the total impression the director wishes the play to create.

The idea of 'frame' was crucial to the insight of the semioticians. It derived, through the Prague School, from the work of de Saussure and Charles Peirce, by which language itself could be regarded as a concrete sign conveying meaning in the same manner as a painting or sculpture. Semioticians conjectured that, by framing any moment of action on stage, they could adduce a science of signs for the theatre. In this manner they could objectively analyse and discuss how the meaning of that moment was produced. The history of the frame in theatre is interesting in itself. As it has come down to us in the proscenium arch, it was essentially borrowed from the painter's art in the Renaissance: put a frame around something and you make it stand out, be more significant than the surrounding space. When stepping on to a stage in a quite empty theatre, there is a feeling that somehow one is being watched – even if only by God. So the semioticians attempted to play God, halt the passing moment of theatre in its tracks, frame it and from the concrete signs thus produced, create a vocabulary of signs by which that moment, and all the interrelated moments of the theatrical event, could be analysed and made to reveal how they produced their mysteries.

If semiotics was not entirely successful in this enterprise – misunderstanding the final, total effect of acting, which is larger than the sum of its parts (signs) – it was a necessary and laudable endeavour. It has energized the contemporary discussion of the need for a theory of performance, to get away from the judgement of theatre, a practical activity, in literary language, and to look for means of discussing performance activities on their own terms – the genesis of this book. So, if we are to spend some further time in looking into something that, finally, doesn't entirely work, it is to help us put the questions of identifying acting in a sharper perspective: to establish ground rules, and to clear the critical underbrush to get a better look at the game.

Semioticians have identified three basic types of signs. First, there are icons, which represent what is signified by a direct image: a box of matches stands for a box of matches; a cigarette stands for a cigarette. Then there are index signs: these are essentially gestural, indicating or moving toward an object or person denominated – signs much used in theatre. Finally there are symbols, where there is no immediately recognizable relationship between the signifier and the signified. Speech is a system of symbolic signs: the sound we make when we say the word 'cat' doesn't approximate to the sound made by a cat, nor does the word, when written, resemble a cat in shape, and yet it is an agreed symbol in the English language. In the French language, the symbol is '*chat*' which becomes a problem for the semioticians: there are no verbal signs that work universally.

The problems that had, since Aristotle, bedevilled the discussion of theatre as a performance activity tended to get in the semiotician's way: the semantic and the phenomenological problems are still there; for even a language of signs is still a language, and theatre happens in real time and space not theoretical time and space. We cannot in practical terms frame a sign in theatre, that is, freeze its action in time to examine it – once it is frozen its nature is changed: we are looking at a tableau not a dramatic action. It is like asking, 'When does acting happen?' This is similar to the semantic problem of where I am when I jump into a river (leaving aside Heraclitus's question as to what a river is). Am I on the bank? No, that is before I have jumped. Am I in the air – no, that is after I have jumped. So the question of what it *is* that we see in the frame remains.

Added to this problem of the moment, there is also the question of deciding who is responsibile for doing what, in which part of that moment. To look at acting we need to tease it out from the cluster of interrelated signs. Yet it can't be what it is at a perceived moment without the supporting signs. At the most fundamental level, leaving aside costume, lighting and settings, Othello's acting is for the most part dependent upon Iago's. Both are in their turn influenced by the audience's responses, and are attempting to support a directorial interpretation. The complex structure of signifiers that makes up a performance is always greater than the sum of its parts, and those parts, being interdependent, can never validly be viewed discretely.

To return to the categories of signs that semioticians have defined, we discover that symbolic meaning can be intentionally or unintentionally attached to any of them. Smoke, for example, at the simplest level is a sign of fire, which symbolizes danger; however, in another context may be taken to mean warmth and comfort. At its most symbolic level, smoke may also indicate the evanescence of human life as it drifts toward the heavens. A watch and chain across an actor's chest may iconically be a sign for itself, a mechanism for telling time, but it may also be a sign of prosperity and, depending upon how it is used by the actor, a sign of an anal personality.

If the meaning of intentional signs has a problem with precision, the fact that the actor is human and subject to the accidents of human existence complicates the problem further. An actor may stub his toe at an entrance and invest the character with a temporary limp. The dropping of a line can make an actor blush or go deathly pale. Any attempt to deal with a human being as data within a scientific system is bound to be flawed.

The interpretation of any sign by an audience will be dependent upon an accepted code of conventions: both theatrical and sociocultural. Both of these codes change all the time, and perception of the external manifestation of what is good acting changes with them. Goethe's rules for his actors in eighteenth-century Weimar, described posture and position on stage according to the characters' rank in society: the person of higher social scale always occupies the right side of the stage. Actors were required never to act in profile or to turn their backs to spectators. A careful, refined set of signs for an essentially verbal drama. Less than a hundred years later, the conventions of melodrama could not have been more different. The villain not only had to wear a precisely signed costume of black cloak, black top hat and black moustache (it is interesting how black has conventionally been a sign of danger and vitality – there is a story from Pepys that Charles II, himself a swarthy individual, once remarked at the theatre, 'Odds Fish, how is it that whenever there is a rogue they clap a black wig on him?'), but had a conventionally choreographed series of actions:

Nancy was always dragged around the stage by her hair, and after this effort Sikes [*sic*] always looked defiantly at the gallery, where he was answered by a loud and fearful curse. . . . The curse was answered by Sikes dragging Nancy twice around the stage and then . . . working up to a well-rehearsed climax, smeared Nancy with red ochre and seemed to dash her brains out on the stage.[1]

The audience's insistence upon its understood convention of signs being fulfilled is further illustrated by the story of the melodrama actor who, inspired by the advent of realism, crumpled to his death on stage, only to be roundly booed by the audience and made to get up and die in the proper manner, arms clasped to his side and falling perpendicularly backwards. There is certainly a problem as to how far what is accepted as 'good' acting is related to the fulfilling of the conventional expectations of a particular time. By contradistinction, an actor who is true to the conventions of a script, which are no longer understood by an audience, may be adjudged a poor actor. This is inevitably a problem with the inherited repertory which will give us a script – a set of written signs – without the physical glossary of signs with which to translate them.

Even if we accept the idea of the primacy of text – the play at least will stand still to be read, and surely that would give it a solid, significative status – there are still problems. Indeed, there have even been attempts to create a system of signs for plots in texts, so that all possible basic structures could be represented in a kind of algebraic formula. But it doesn't help us much to know that all dramatic structures have concrete bases when, in their performance, an infinite number of permutations may be played upon the signs. Good dramatic texts, by definition, have spaces and silences within their written structure which, when filled by the actor on stage, will have different dynamics according to the creativity of the actor. Comedy and farce in particular rely upon this physical illustration of the text in action. Also Shakespeare's work, due to the open and scenically sparse nature of his stage, demanded a good deal of iconic and deitic gesture to establish his situation.

In theatre, gesture and movement rule over words. One only has to look at how far the influence of television has triumphed over reading to accept how strong and direct the physical image, or sign, is: and many potential signs are operating at any one time within the stage frame. In some respects, the actor, although essentially the most significant and dynamic sign, is merely the tip of the iceberg; to use a somewhat better image, the stage event is an edifice, built upon a base of multifarious signs which are synthesized and condensed into others, which make signs with larger meanings until the edifice becomes the total *mise-en-scène*, or *mise-en*-sign. The actor, within the context of the whole of this, is trying to get the audience to look at a particular sign at a particular moment and interpret it in a particular way. To trace the process backwards and, hopefully, both to clarify it and put it in a total perspective: the pointing of an actor's finger, a simple deitic sign, is part of an arm, in the sleeve of a jacket, which is part of a costume that has a particular style and colour (iconic signs which are symbolic), which is part of a stage design that includes that costume among many others, plus whatever physical environment creates the set. All of which are both iconic and potentially symbolic signs, i.e. they have potentially more than one meaning. Thus, the interpretation of the simple deitic finger sign on the part of the actor is informed in its meaning by all the other elements on the stage at that time and, if that were not complicated enough, the very nature of the stage space itself – be it proscenium, thrust, arena, indoor, outdoor, etc. – will also have an effect upon the way in which the audience will interpret the actor's simple sign. Indeed, before the actor even gets to act, maybe even before he or she is cast, a whole host of predetermined signifiers have already been at work: set design, costume design, director's interpretation, not to mention the producer's budget which will have a determining effect on all of the above. So, to adduce a precise and specific sign for the tip of the actor's index finger and the deitic sign it creates, which, we have seen, is merely the tip of a whole concatenation of signs, gives some sense of the task the semioticians set themselves.

Certainly one of the functions of art is to condense, focus, highlight and generally organize the miasmic chaos of reality. The director's function is to ensure that the actor creates – from the impulses coming at him from the text, in the context of the costume, set and other surrounding signs – the sign that at that moment in the play's journey best conveys the director's intention to the audience. But it can never be guaranteed; and the way in which the audience decodes any one sign, will be in the light of all the other stimuli it is receiving or has received. This, quite apart from the fact that even the simplest act, sitting, is fraught with possibilities – because of the frame, all stage actions are *sign*ificant – one cannot just sit, or do 'nothing' on stage. One is doing nothing for a purpose – in order not to do something else, which in itself becomes a sign.

Theatre performance is a highly complex mimesis, and any one sign will retain the multifarious possibilities that all other signs have fed into it. This gives some small idea of the difficulty the semioticians undertook in creating a vocabulary of signs that will have the same specific and objective meaning for all members of the audience; even for the most unsophisticated member who will give the actor the praise and blame for whatever experience the audience has.

If this were not enough there is, beyond the mass of signifiers bombarding the audience at any one moment during the passage of the play, what might be termed a gestalt sign. This carries the overall 'meaning' of the production, above and beyond the possible meanings of all the signifiers the audience will decode during the performance. The stage is a metaphor for the world, and by putting a frame around the events of the real world it cannot escape enhancing the metaphorical meaning of that world: harvest, nurture, continuance, communality become metaphorical images within the stage world. A sunrise, or a baby, becomes a metaphor of new beginnings, new hope. The Hymen at the end of the Greek comedy is still with us as the young lovers of our dramas, now on film, walk hand in hand into the eternal sunset. It is this capacity for turning life into poetry that is at the basis of all art, and is incorporated by mimesis into theatre. On the stage the actor all too easily becomes a metaphor for himself, like Macbeth's 'poor player' who 'struts and frets his hour upon the stage'. The actor saying these words about the actor on the world's stage that man is, becomes his own metaphor while revealing himself as a man within the character of Macbeth:[2] levels of signs which may not be decoded equally by all members of the audience.

Perhaps one of the most problematical signs, encompassing the metaphorical meaning of a play, comes from our modern theatre. At the end of Brecht's play, *Mother Courage*,[3] the name-character is reduced to pulling her own wagon, having lost all her children and much of her livelihood in following the war. Brecht's intention through this image, or sign or *gestus*, was that the audience should take a political view of Courage's circumstances and see how her lack of a correct perception of the situation had allowed her to be abused by a military-capitalist society and so reduced to the level of a beast of burden. Brecht thus sought to raise the audience's political consciousness against the military-capitalist ethos. However, instinct for metaphor tended to make the audience take a humanistic view of the sign and applaud the irrepressible nature of the human spirit and humankind's capacity to triumph over adversity.

Again, from the modern theatre, *Waiting for Godot* (perhaps in aesthetic and existential terms, the most *avant-garde* play of the 1950s) was seen by Marxists to be advocating inaction, therefore supporting the political status quo, and was thus judged by them as 'reactionary'. The total sign of the play was thus subject to quite opposed decodings. So, while the semiotic concept can be a useful tool in teaching an audience member to look at the vast range of signs which go to make up the effect of a theatrical performance, and especially to break the suspension of disbelief which can impose the simplistic criterion of external reality upon the stage event, it still has many inadequacies in terms of any objective consideration of the art of theatre or craft of acting.

The major problem with the attempt at achieving a precise semiotic vocabulary is the phenomenological one that behind the sign of the actor remains a real human being – with all the subjectivity that presupposes – who has become a sign for an imaginary human being, who has his or her own reality within the context of the play. One of the excitements of theatre is the tension between the self of the actor and the fictional self of the character. Just as it has been said that the language on the page of the script must on stage be 'co-meddled with the blood', so will a sign have emotional potentiality which encourages subjective interpretation or decoding. Simple identification, as Genet has said, is the 'lowest form of appreciation'.

If this problem for semiotics arises when looking at the actor alone on stage, it is easily compounded when the actor is placed within the sociocultural conventions of a time and the aesthetic conventions of a scenic space. And, however useful the semiotic effort may be as a critical catalyst and tool for hermeneutics, even if an agreed system of signs were possible, it would still smack of the sterile. It would reduce the actor to the *Über-Marionette* so dear to the heart of Gordon Craig, and would change the very nature

of theatrical art: born of poetry, theatre would be reduced to a
science and available to discussion only within the closed system
its vocabulary of signs allowed.

Chapter 3

Acting and athletics

Accepting, then, the fact that theatre is a living art; constantly on the move even while it is being framed; whose spontaneity is part of its very attraction; and whose mirroring of the multifarious parts of life makes it impossible to trap and objectify as the semioticians would wish: what can we look at in our attempt to say what acting is?

Well, the actor's body is the fundamental sign. When it is there it is looked at, and when it moves it attracts the audience's attention. And it is the way in which that body moves that communicates the nature of the action to the audience. Drama, Aristotle told us, is the imitation of an action. Not the imitation of an emotion or of a psyche, but of an action, and we recognize the nature of that action by its physical form. The impulse to action may be emotional or psychological, but the expression of it, to be communicable, must be in an enacted form. Now it is true that action and activity in the sense of movement are not necessarily the same. As we saw in the previous sections, because of the frame, to do nothing on stage is an action, or to use the semiotician's term, a sign. It is, in fact, one of the more difficult things for an actor to do well, both because there is no apparent focus of concentration outside the actor, and because of the need for intensity of energy to keep the audience's interest in the motionless figure. Consequently, there is very little time on stage when doing nothing can be sustained for long; movement, the performance of some kind of activity which creates an action, tends to be the norm.

The actor's body in movement, playing actions, making points, is fundamental to theatre. Bodies in movement, playing their kind

of actions, and making/scoring their kind of points is also how we
look at games or sporting activities. And at a very basic level, an
actor is a player, and acting is an athletic activity. When we look
at athletes, we are usually watching what it is they did to achieve
their objective. Did they beat their man? Did they get their pass
to a fellow player? Did they score a run/goal/point? This is the
equivalent in acting of: Did the actor play the action in at least
a manner which took the plot in the necessary direction, and
beyond that in an interesting or surprising way? It is more difficult
to judge success in acting because there is no other man to beat
(the other actor is complicit in his or her defeat); no ball to reach
the other player, or go into the net, or cross the boundary line.
Actors are to some degree their own goal, they 'score' themselves.
The interest lies in *how* they achieve the goal, not *if* they do, which
is a given. You may be a successful and effective player of certain
games without being an attractive player (a kick-and-rush player
as it was called in soccer): this seems not to be the case with
acting.

If we were to take our eye off the ball for a moment and look
at the player, we could see what he or she were doing in order to
be effective, how the body was working to achieve the aim, and
possibly what makes one player more attractive than another to
watch – even if both are effective. I have already mentioned Gulagong in tennis; there are players that come to mind in every sport,
just as actors come to mind. With actors, it is the body we are
watching all the time: they are their own instrument. There is no
bat, no ball; no piano or violin; no paintbrush or sculptor's knife
of other art forms. As athletes, actors are possibly closer to divers
and gymnasts, whose bodies are their own instruments. Though
here again there is an agreement on the specifics of the form these
athletes are to achieve which, to the semiotician's dismay, is not
the case in theatre.

The point is, however, whether we are speaking of the athlete's
body or the actor's body, there is, besides the achievement of the
goal (making the fulfilling of the objective the actor's goal) the
physical manner in which this is done – and the qualities we may
examine tend to be similar in both game-playing and acting.
Acting is an athletic activity. The grace and skill of the athlete is
described in such terms as balance, power, timing, agility, fluidity;
and these terms may equally be applied to the actor's body as it

moves in space, encumbered though it may be with costume. Indeed, the very way in which an actor can make the costume seem part of his or her body is an indication of physical skill.

It is often charged against actors that they do not continue to train for their profession on a regular basis as dancers do at the barre and musicians at their scales. There is some truth in this, though it is certainly my experience, at least among American actors, in this post-Grotowski and personal health-conscious period, that the two venues actors playing the regions immediately seek are the local bars and the local gyms! It is, in fact, not possible for actors to have a long and successful career without paying attention to their physical condition. At a very basic level, acting is hard labour; it takes enormous energy to sustain something twice your size and pitch it to the back of a 2,000-seat house, and do this six times a week and twice on Thursdays and Saturdays, or whatever. And, here, we are talking about an average role. When one gets into the frenetic activity of farce, or some of the major classical roles, working as a ditchdigger seems child's play by comparison. One of the classic theatre jokes is: 'What do you need most to be able to play *Lear*?' Answer: 'A light Cordelia.' An image that has stuck with me from once playing the Button Moulder in *Peer Gynt*. By the time Peer reaches the Button Moulder he has clambered over mountains, been pursued by Trolls, shipwrecked on the high seas and run the gamut of an insane asylum. It was an outdoor, night-time performance, and out of the lights this figure tottered towards me, wig awry and spiked from the sweat that was also running down his cheeks, making livid scars on his makeup. He stank of onion and was taking huge gulps of air, alternately swelling and shrinking as he gasped out his lines. He seemed a cross between a ghost and a witch doctor. He had been through the circus ring of the ritual and the emotional wringer of the performance, and the pain was palpable. Like a marathon runner at the end of the race, only the fortitude and desire of the athlete were driving him on to the goal: through the applause to the dressing room where the shower and the drink were waiting.

More than sustaining the sheer physical endurance of acting, the actor's body is also the repository of the role. It is in muscular memory that the learning of a part takes place. This is no different from the learning of any other physical activity on the part of the human being. As a child we learn to walk downstairs by repeating the activity until we get it right. So with acting. And, just as later in life, if we think about what we are doing to walk downstairs we will probably stumble, so with acting: if we think about what we are doing, we will trip – over the line probably.

The French acknowledge this process by their word for a rehearsal: *répétition*. The term 'rehearsal' gives us away somewhat with its connotation of saying again, an emphasis upon the verbal aspect of theatre. It is not in the mind but in muscular memory that a performance is stored. And, in complementary fashion, it is from the muscular memory that the impulses to action derive. As with walking downstairs, we absorb physical reactions to all our experience of life, and it is from this huge store of experiential memories that the actor draws the impulses towards action that create the part. Even the somewhat tendentious 'emotion memory' process of the Method was based on the rediscovery of the physical circumstances of a situation, which then catalyse the impulsive reactions to those circumstances. It is the way in which these impulses are arranged that creates the rhythm of a performance, the rhythm that an actor rides on which pulls him or her through, and which, if missing, makes the evening seem like trying to balance upon a greasy log in a river; or like pushing a huge rock uphill.

Patently, for these impulses to flow as efficiently as possible, all the channels in the actor's body must be open. This is really what is meant by relaxation. The actor should not let tension get in the way of the free response of the body's impulsive reaction. It is not the flaccid, spaced-out relaxation of some of the meditative philosophies of the 1960s, but the balanced and focused relaxation of the athlete at the start of a race. For the actor, the spine is the crucial element. Not only is the spine the main perpendicular in the human body, and thus fundamental in distinguishing our posture from that of other animals, but it is the main channel of the nervous system in distributing impulses throughout the body. A free and flexible spine is a fundamental requirement for the actor; and the area in the body where the spine meets the pelvis, the area of the solar plexus, is the crucial centre of the actor's work. Not only is this the major crossroads of the body and determines its balance, but it is a major centre of nerve endings and, in the diaphragm, of the breath. Breath, nervous impulse and balance are all here in the actor's working centre.

Respiration, aspiration, inspiration, spirit, all have the same stem and are integrated here in the actor's centre. The way in which an actor is centred will have much to do with his or her ability. By balance we mean that the body's weight and energy are related in such a way that the body is able to follow any impulse in any direction without a noticeable pause between impulse and act. A simple test of this potential in an actor is the discovery of optimal leg spacing while standing: if a slight push can set the actor off balance, then the leg spacing is too close and the actor will betray weakness in holding spaces; if a slight push meets solid resistance, the actor is probably too far spaced, too planted on the ground and will require too much effort to respond to an impulse – he will seem to be acting after the beat. Of course, as we shall see when we talk about an actor's process, the actor will adjust the stance according to the balance of the character, its strengths and weaknesses. It is in such physical ways that character may be created. But, in order for this to happen, the actor will need his or her own instrument to be at optimum capacity for playing, in other words, to be as well tuned as possible. And, just as when we know that a musical instrument is out of tune, or that an athlete has beautiful balance – Walter Payton the American football player was even nicknamed 'sweetness' because of the grace of his movement – so with an actor. The capacity for instant, powerful, controlled reaction is a recognizable attribute of acting.

When acting was still a popular outdoor activity, closer to bear-baiting and the fairground, the physicality of the actor was a palpable presence, and a recognizable athleticism was a given. Perhaps the *Commedia dell'Arte* and the theatre of Shakespeare saw the last of this tradition; before theatre went indoors and took on the mantle of bourgeois respectability and sentiment in the eighteenth century. From this time right through the encroachment of psychological naturalism, the idea of actors as skilled athletes became lost as they tried more and more to hide their skills behind the pretence that they were not special beings but just everyday people you could find behind the wall of the house next door. Skill in handling cups of tea and coffee and the domestic paraphernalia of naturalism lessened the sense of athletic demands as being part of the game of acting. This is not to say that athletic attributes were not still part of the equipment of the actor, but they were clothed in much less evident form.

The return to athleticism in acting probably began with Meyerhold and his conscious use of the physical form of the actor, trained through his physical technique of biomechanics. This was carried further in the post-Artaudian period of the 1960s and 1970s, especially by directors such as Joseph Chaikin, Peter Brook and Jerzy Grotowski. With the movement away from language as social discourse or psychological disclosure, towards the creation of powerful signs of 'signals through the flames', the actor as athlete came back into his own. Images remain with us from this time: the agonized athleticism of Ryszard Cieslak in *The Constant Prince*; the insane contortions of the inmates in the *Marat/Sade*, with Glenda Jackson using herself as a whip with which to flagellate de Sade; the collective expulsions of Richard Schechner's actors at the birth of Dionysus in his adaptation of *The Bacchae*. All of these images, actions, signals and signs demanded great athleticism from the actors.

The training of these actors was itself an athletic activity. Grotowski, particularly, codified a regimen of exercises geared to the attaining of the very qualities we have suggested as necessary to the athlete: balance, timing, agility, power, plasticity. These exercises activated body memory and made its store of memories immediately accessible. Our tissue and nerves have remembered, and will respond again to similar stimuli: do the act and the feeling will follow. Such a physical approach returned to the biomechanical theories of Meyerhold, and incorporated those of William James and Moshe Feldenkrais: the actor's vocabulary of memories is stored in physical form. Every emotion in one way or another is associated and linked in the cortex with some muscular configuration and attitude that has the power of reinstating the dynamics of a situation.

Balance is fundamental to athlete and actor. The ability at all times to have one's centre related to the ball, or action, so that one can do whatever task is required: score a goal, pass the ball, make a moment, say a line with the necessary dynamics and effortless appearance. Timing is a function of controlled balance. It is the adjustment of pace to wrong-foot an opponent; the holding of the word, to frame it with time and space, before hitting it for six.

All of these athletic attributes are necessary to the actor. They won't all be demanded in the same degree in all parts. But even when not called upon in a virtuoso way, such as Olivier's great fall in *Coriolanus*, their presence gives grace or lack of it to simply lighting a cigarette or sitting in a chair. And it is the integrating of all these techniques in the balanced centre that distinguishes the art that disguises art. On a good shot, a tennis player's racket will seem simply an extension of the body; on less good shots the effort involved is apparent. It is a similar attribute of the actor which, in the heat of a performance, makes good acting seem to disappear; the actor is totally absorbed in the action of the moment; it is only if we consciously suspend our suspension of disbelief that we can see the moment being made, and have to remind ourself of the qualities which made it disappear.

There is one further attribute of the actor's athleticism, and that is the response it brings from the audience: an aspect of the pleasure the audience receives from performance, the appreciation of skill. The vicarious enjoyment by the audience of a level of human possibility being explored which, on a day-to-day basis, is beyond their reach. The skill of the athlete is evident, and can be measured in runs or goals scored, in record times set. This skill is present with the actor too, despite the run-of-the-mill perception that acting is easy. It is not only the artist's aim to make it look easy, but the omnipresence of 'realistic' evaluation has taught the audience to make judgements in mundane terms. In spite of this, the audience is aware when they are in the presence of an extraordinary skill or talent and takes pleasure in 'assisting' at the performance. We cannot all climb Everest, run four-minute miles, kick fifty-yard goals, or play Macbeth or King Lear, but there is a great deal of pleasure to be had from the knowledge that we are part of a species that can; and there is a physical thrill to be had from the sharing in the experience of an athlete or actor, whose extraordinary ability can make the occasion live for us.

Chapter 4

The psychology of acting

'This is no life for a grown-up person.' This remark has been attributed to various well-known actors who, in a moment of clarity, crouched in the dark at ten o'clock at night, their faces scrawled with makeup, have waited to launch themselves upon a brilliantly lit stage where, with nowhere to hide, they must flaunt their persons in some probably absurd manner before the acclaim or displeasure of hundreds of people, who at least think they are grown-up.

Why then do actors do it? For fame and fortune, the Break, the eternal optimism of humankind that has got it this far. Possibly. Certainly the reality, the statistics do not support that as sole motive. About 70 per cent of the acting profession is out of work at any one time, and about 30 per cent of the acting profession makes a living wage at acting alone. So, for every Richard Burton and Elizabeth Taylor, there are a hundred actors in line at the unemployment office, and a hundred more waiting to stand and serve them in any restaurant in which they might want to sit down.

So what is it then? Is an actor a *lusus naturae*, one of the many little jokes God plays on humankind? Is it a genetic quirk that obliges actors to follow their star? Is there a psychological profile that marks actors off from their fellows? There is certainly a stereo-typical opinion of the actor that seems to support the insight of our iconic actor, that it is not a way of life for a mature person. Actors are somehow irresponsible children who refuse to grow up and have no identity of their own. By definition, to have to pretend to be someone else for a living casts some doubt upon who you are, and is less than a recommendation of reliability.

The obligatory phenomenological dichotomy seems to catch the actor out again. The very lifestyle suggests a split personality. Mask and face, self and character, the actor seems to live a life of contradictions, to be pulled in opposite directions: inwardly searching, outwardly giving; in need of an audience, in fear of an audience; a childlike freedom, and an adult responsibility; an adulated artist and a miserable pimp. These forces pulling in opposite directions could easily suggest that the actor has indeed not matured, lacks a defined core of self; a personal ego.

In a certain perspective, acting can be seen as a search for the self, a personal quest that actors have externalized and formalized through the many roles they can play. These can be seen as the possible testing of many selves without, perhaps, having to take responsibility for any one of them. Whether the actor is a child, it is certain that an actor needs to be able to retain some of the fantastical imagination, and freedom of action to test the world by playing, that is part of the development of every child. Perhaps one of the attractions of acting is that the actor is licensed to do on stage what is forbidden in 'normal' society. More than this, it often gains the approval of that society: something important to the developing ego. It is gaining a place in the world without having to operate on the world's terms. To be able to enact a script that is already written gives a certain security in the midst of all the contradictions of existence. Acting may be an escape from the harshness of the superego and a licence to continue to give play to the creative energy of the libido long after the normal world would have suppressed this into acceptable channels.

These possible psychological perspectives can all be looked at in more than one way. The desire to be the centre of attention could be seen as narcissistic and yet the fear involved in this exposure may be a positive part of a rite of passage, a need for actors to prove themselves, a journey through fear, necessary to create a wholeness, through the performance, in the divided self. The actor's authenticity and vitality may depend upon the integrity of the performing self – the more dynamic it is, the more the ego is defined. In some sense, the audience may be responsible for creating the actor's ego, it holds together the splits. The actor, ironically, may only be him- or herself (despite being the character) when performing. Actors may need the constant state of anxiety that performing induces, to prove they exist. On the other hand, this anxiety and stress can produce stage fright at the possibility that the performing self isn't going to work, and then the actor won't be there, or will be naked, or will have forgotten the lines, or be in the wrong costume: all manifestations of anxiety which suggest the lack of a self when the stage manifestation fails.

The rehearsal period follows the pattern of self-development. There is the early, playful, experimental period of discovery; the taking of risks because the existential risk is not yet great: the learning period. Then there is what might be termed the adolescence, when the actor wants to stand on his or her own feet, to begin the withdrawal from the paternal or maternal support of the director, yet still needs support. The actor is resentful of personal inadequacies, with his or her own lack of facility with lines and moves; likewise resentful of the director who now seems to be judging and watching this stumbling performance, which the actor knows isn't complete. Then, finally, the hoped-for adulthood, the integrated and confident performer, self-secure in lines, moves, who can treat the director as an equal adult and present the newly created self for the admiration of the audience world.

The psychology of rehearsal may also be looked at in Freudian terms. There is an oral period when everything is fodder for the actor; everything goes into the actor's maw to be chewed and tasted and the director's function is nurturing. Then there is the anal period, the accepting of a structure of blocking, the learning of lines, the necessary routine of the rehearsal, the socialization of the give and take with fellow actors. Here the director has a disciplinary role.

There is a strong phallic potentiality in acting, an erotic relationship to the audience. This also has a connection to stage fright with fear of impotence or castration by the director's necessary withdrawal and the potential withholding of audience approval. There is clearly sexual imagery in the language of performance: the fear of a 'flop', the hope the audience will 'love it'. It is probably most strongly manifested today in the rock concert, where the guitar is used phallically to bring the audience to a pitch of orgasmic excitement.

This potentiality for reaching the height of adulation, and at the same time being faced with the fear of failure – the inability to 'perform' – is what creates both a strong sense of mutual support and a strong sense of ironical self-criticism on the part of actors.

The dressing room is a place where actors are all implicitly mutually self-supporting against the common enemy. The physical closeness of the acting community underlines this need for support. The embraces after readings and auditions, often between actors who have only just met, is an acknowledgement of shared trials; of the worship of the same cruel gods. And the knowledge that these gods may lift you up one night only to cast you down the next; that what is always on the actor's mind is the hope of the next job – all this leads to a self-deprecating irony, a sharing of the realization that finally it is all a trick, that you may be found out at any moment, that the audience may all have gone home. Peter O'Toole has said that the character in Beckett's *Waiting for Godot* was called Lucky because he had no words in the second act – nothing to learn, and not too much to go wrong. Roger Rees has said that an actor's favourite time is between being offered a part and the first read-through. This is the time to bathe in the glow of acceptance before the danger of being thrown to the dogs. A joke about dogs reveals an ironical self-knowledge on the part of actors. There were three dogs: a philosopher's dog, a mathematician's dog and an actor's dog. Each was given a pile of bones. The philosopher's dog arranged the bones in a circle and ran around it whining; the mathematician's dog arranged the bones in series and growled at anyone who approached; the actor's dog ate all the bones, fucked the other two dogs, and asked if he could go home early.

The 'actor-police' are always present in the dressing room, to keep in place any actor whose histrionic flair might be getting out of hand. An actor will dab a touch of rouge onto his proboscis and leave for the stage saying mildly, 'I think I'll try a little nose acting tonight.' An actor playing two parts will return to the dressing room saying, 'I nearly dislocated my neck tonight. I couldn't remember whether it was shoulders hunched for Westmoreland and sloped for Northumberland or the other way around, and got stuck in the middle.' Gallows humour all. A necessary perspective in a rewarding but cruel – another dichotomy – profession. The knowledge that while performing is the most important thing in the world to the actor, that any moment it may all be taken away, and the psychological preparation for the breadline must always lie just beneath the surface of any present success.

The adult tends to gain a certain security in finding a place in society. The actor tends to face the child's fear of rejection through-out his or her life. With this rejection, implicitly by adult society, comes the freedom not to have to subscribe to all the mores of that society and the licence to 'act' in a manner that might be thought irresponsible by that society, or, at least, to give rein to his or her instincts in public and on the public stage in a way that most members of society have been trained not to do. So there is probably a necessary truth in the social perception of the actor as a child, an immature person with the irresponsibility of an ill-formed ego, or an ill-formed sense of social self.

Certainly, some highly visible members of the acting profession have found it difficult to distinguish between the licence society gives them as actors in a controlled situation, and a licence to act out their personal problems in public. If the actor is undeveloped as a professional, the self-indulgence and irresponsibility of the childish ego can take over and produce a public persona that is sometimes temporarily lauded for its attractive 'rebel' status. Of course, this does make good copy; especially when the rebel dies young in a car accident.

There is, however, a difference between remaining psychologi-cally childish throughout one's life, and the ability to retain child-like instincts. The childish actor could not survive in a tough profession. The ability to sustain the constant rejections of the career in fact requires a strong sense of self, a strong ego that can take the rejection as part of a professional process and not a rejection of the individual as a human being. One of the more difficult tasks for young professionals is to be able to show their wares, pimp for oneself, and to feel neither cheapened by the process nor personally rejected by failure to get the part. And there comes a time in the career of all except the few immediate stars, when actors have to decide if they are ever going to be 'quite right' for the part, to face up to the possibility that the talent may not be there. Then the actor has to decide whether to leave the profession or whether a life as an out-of-work actor is a life enough. For some it is. For others it is the way to self-destruction, as the necessary childlike vulnerability never achieves the support of the professional ego.

The need for vulnerability to succeed and toughness to survive: another of the constant contradictions that can tear the actor apart. Vulnerability is necessary to allow the actor access to childlike, not childish, instincts. An unfortunate part of the process of becoming adult is, for most people, the building of strong defences against the toughness of the world. As we accommodate ourselves to social approval and don the straitjacket of adult behaviour, so we lose the ability to play in the sense that we had as a child, when playing was instinctual, a part of our exploration of the world and of our own capacity in relationship to it.

The adult world is enlarged in practical scope but tends to be limited in imagination, and predictable in response. In the known lies safety; in the controlled lies acceptance. Part of the actor's function is to continue to explore the unknown and to discover the unpredictable. This is done through play. Play is a release of energy that tests the bounds of the possible, of reality. Sixty- and seventy-year-old actors still have the instinct to play, if they did not they would not have survived thus far as actors. And, because play isn't a normal activity in the adult world, actors have to be licensed by society to do it. Most people tend to work to control their instincts as they go through life, not to release actions that would upset the adult applecart. Actors are sanctioned and encouraged to do this. It is a vicarious pleasure for the adult audience, trapped by the straight and narrow path through the pitfalls of existence, the moment of atrophy is held at bay by the actor's playful triumph over the paralysing demands of adulthood, and by the revelation that the possibilities of childhood still exist.

Actors cannot be judged by standards of 'normality'. They are required to confront, on our behalf, the very quick of life which is too painful or too powerful to be lived with day by day. They release the interior scream of tragedy or anarchic bray of comedy. To do this, they must live in a psychic modality that is other than a norm. The actor has to be a little 'mad' to inhabit certain histrionic realms. But the trick is to know that you are and when you are. It is a controlled schizophrenia that manages to reconcile all the contradictions that an actor has to live with. In some respect the ability to touch madness and to control it helps to keep the actor sane. Though touched by instinct, it is revealed by skill and controlled by technique. With the destructive capacity to touch human pain and anguish comes a certain freedom, the power to release it. Out of the destructive power comes artistic experience. Actors are obliged to confront what most human beings cannot afford to admit to: they drop the social pretence of 'nor-

mality', 'sanity', and transmute what they discover in the underlying slime into art. To balance, again that word, on the tightrope
between normality and madness is how the actor controls the
necessary schizophrenia. The neurosis is part of the technique of
the art.

To continue to be an actor, this balance must be maintained.
To fall off on one side is to take off the motley and accept the
triumph of the limitations of adulthood. To fall off on the other
is to lose the grasp of the professional ego and confuse the two
realities the actor 'acts' within. In watching a child at play, one
is always aware of the complete merging of playfulness with
seriousness. This doubling capacity is the essence of the professional actor's schizophrenia. Children need no such technique.
They can play tinker, tailor, soldier, sailor and return to themselves in an instant, without ever being aware of the duplicity. For
adults to be someone else and yet retain their own integrity they
must be childlike but be more than a child: they must be conscious
artists.

Chapter 5

The psychology in acting

From the psychology of the actor we turn to the much-discussed issue of the use of psychology in the acting process. One of the major problems in dealing, today, with the nature of acting is that we are the immediate inheritors of the sensibility of the naturalistic period, when a comparison with the lineaments of an external reality became a popular criterion for the judgement of acting. This has become the more entrenched as the spread of film and television has brought 'acting' into the living rooms of virtually every member of society. Thus the necessary conventions of a *theatrical* experience, whereby one goes to a particular place at a particular time to witness an event that, although part of the spectator's total life experience, has its own particular identity, have been lost. Television now brings 'acting', intermixed with the 'real' life of news and talk shows and interviews, and the sales-pitch pseudo-sincerity of commercials into the undifferentiated consciousness of everyone, as they eat their evening meal and flick from channel to channel.

This exposure of acting, both to the generic *mélange* of media conventions, and the judgement of popular critical taste, is a fairly recent development in the long history of acting as a human cultural endeavour. Since Plato condemned actors for being hypocrites and a threat to the state, much discussion of theatre up through the Renaissance was in literary terms based upon the 'nature' of the dramatic effect rather than the actor's 'achievement' of that effect. If acting as a process was considered, it was based upon the vocabulary of humours as a guide to human identity, and the expectations imposed upon human action by the rules of social decorum. It was the eighteenth century, with the growth of the enquiring conscience of the Enlightenment and the beginnings of the spread of literacy, that saw the first serious attempts in print to set out the nature of the acting process.

The Hills, John and Aaron, were perhaps the first seriously to attempt to define the actor's ways and means, and they did this by integrating the sentimental sensibility of the later eighteenth century with the structure of neoclassical rules. To the idea of a set of conventional gestures which conveyed the image of the various human passions to the audience, the Hills added that necessity of the sentimental period, the connection of passion and feeling. Thereby, the actor's imagination conceives a strong idea of the passion which then impresses its form upon the face and muscles of the body. Although the vocabulary of conventional gestures was still a basis of acting style, the Hills could suggest that the gesture, strictly speaking, was not conventional at all but that 'the formal expression follows ineluctably from the active conception of one of the inherently dramatic passions'.[1]

However, much as the Hills might protest the idea of strict conventionality, it was an accepted tenet of the time that: 'The natural signs of emotion . . . being nearly the same in all men form a universal language which no difference of tribe, no diversity of tongue can darken or render doubtful.'[2] So we are still very much in a neoclassical sensibility, and not too far from the Middle Ages in the determining concept of the humours, and character typicality. Even an Elizabethan book on the art of rhetoric set down received character determinations: a man of good years would be sober, wise, and circumspect; a woman babbling and inconstant; a soldier a great bragger; a courtier flattering; while the English were known for feeding and changing apparel, the Dutch for drinking, the French for pride, and so forth. What the eighteenth-century scribes are doing, is to connect the tradition of acting they inherited to the pervasive idea of the necessity of benevolent feelings which obtained in the period of sentimentality. The interrelating of the social and theatrical sensibility of the period held that the external appearances of the passions – joy, grief, anger, etc. – formed a universal language that led straight from the heart. The signs were natural (i.e. taken from nature) and all agreed on them. They conveyed emotions to the audience, producing a benevolent response.

The classic work of the eighteenth century was Diderot's *Le*

Paradoxe sur le comédien (1830),[3] in which he took up a position very different from the Hills, and very different from the great English actor of the day, David Garrick. Diderot is similarly concerned for the function of gesture in acting. He agreed with the English theorists that words alone could not completely realize dramatic meaning and that they needed to be fleshed out in action and gesture. But Diderot distinguished between gesture and feeling. He argued that an actor's feelings were irrelevant to the passion conveyed by the gestures. Communication for Diderot was a matter of 'rendering so exactly the outward signs of feeling' that the audience was affected by the impact upon their emotions of the recognizable sign, i.e. gesture, of passion. The actor's task, for Diderot, was not connecting the gesture with the passion, but refining the representation of the gesture so that it would have the most direct impact.

Diderot called for a cool head, profound judgement and an exquisite taste as the bases of the actor's technique. It should not be thought that the opposing neoclassical camp was asking for the actor to reveal personal feelings in the role. What Garrick's actor does is to use the accepted vocabulary of gestures to stimulate the audience's emotional response, and find within himself the feeling equivalent to the gesture to help sustain it. There is no sense of any pursuit of personal authenticity. It was not until the romantic period was well advanced that the concept of self, and the ethical idea that the actor, as ethical human being, shouldn't violate his or her own integrity, brought into aesthetic focus the phenomenological issue we discussed earlier of who the actor is when on stage. William Archer's *Masks or Faces* (1888) deals, as the title suggests, with how far the actor reveals him- or herself in the role.[4] It is the beginning of the modern distinction between 'emotional' and 'technical' actors: the feelers and nonfeelers that became an issue for popular debate in the 1940s and 1950s, when the Method was beamed through the success of certain movie stars into the public eye.

Before the Method, however, William Archer and the nineteenth-century French actor Constant Coquelin had set out the opposed positions. The burden of Archer's argument, which is substantiated by the responses he marshals from many of his contemporary actors such as Salvini and Forbes-Robertson, suggests that the actor does not simply use feelings (i.e. create a mask), but reveals his or her face in performance. 'Real' feeling from the actor's expressive self informs the performance, and the actor uses his or her own identity as a channel for the role.

Coquelin put the opposite case for the emotionally disengaged actor: 'I am convinced that one can only be a great actor on the condition of complete self-mastery and ability to express feelings which are not experienced.'[5] Much of Coquelin's discussion describes the actor as a kind of *bricoleur* – a Jack of all trades, or handyman – who picks up experiences on the journey through life and then uses whatever is necessary to play any particular part. While rejecting pure emotional display as the basic quality of acting, Coquelin somehow suggests that there is in an actor a selfhood that is prior to feeling, that maintains its integrity while informing all the actor's work. Coquelin counters the argument of moralistic critics who suggest that actors deny their dignity by pandering their own character to take on the trappings of a dozen others, and are therefore not trustworthy representatives of humankind, by saying that whether emotionally engaged or disengaged, masked or unmasked, an actor does not renounce selfhood, but uses it to give creative dynamics to the role.

By the late nineteenth century, therefore, the lines were drawn as if awaiting the advent of Stanislavski, who was to be the first individual to attempt to systematize the actor's process, rather than simply theorize about its nature. Two immediate factors stand out when looking at Stanislavski's approach. The first is that it was an attempt to set out a systematic acting process in a scientific manner. The second is that, at least in the first instance, its major concern was not with gesture but with inner process. To understand this approach at this particular time (the late nineteenth and early twentieth centuries), we have to go back to where we started with the Hills – to the Enlightenment. One of the major practical results of Enlightenment curiosity was the development of scientific enquiry into the nature of humankind and the universe in which it lived. The scientific principle led to the development of nineteenth-century industry and, from the development of the external world, turned to study the internal workings of the human being itself. Thus to Freud, and the development of psychology at the end of the nineteenth century which placed motivation for human actions deep within the newly significant human psyche.

From this sensibility, Stanislavski drew the scientific nature of his system; the concern for the inner emotional process of human beings, and the principle of subtext: the truth of human motivation did not necessarily appear on the surface of words or actions. The concern for and enquiry into the nature of the human self was also reinforced by the political consequences of the Enlightenment, the benevolence of which – the belief in and concern for the inherent goodness of humanity – led to the sensibility of the romantic period. Romanticism, based then upon the subjectivity of feeling rather than upon classical objectivity of form has, as a necessary concomitant, the desire to allow the feelings of the individual to be expressed, to free him or her from oppressive or restrictive forms of any nature. Thus, the free expression of the desires and feelings of the individual becomes the essential dynamic of human action. The American and French revolutions are the most exemplary expressions of this desire for the freedom of the individual; and further revolutions during the nineteenth century led to the breakup of large empires and the overthrowing of aristocratic and hierarchically structured forms of government in favour of more democratic forms: governments of, for, and by the people.

So, by the end of the nineteenth century, the focus of human concern and enquiry increasingly centred upon the democratic individual seen as the proper and basic unit of emotional, social and political life. In terms of human cultural development, this sensibility brought about the period of realism in the arts; whereby the detailed depiction, both in terms of environment and psychological drive, of the individual leading an everyday life in society became the concern of the drama. No longer classical kings and mythological heroes, not even the manners and mores of the gentry and bourgeoisie; but the 'real' life of the average or 'common' man or woman as it might be perceived by removing a wall of an average house in an average town and looking in. Drama was to concern itself with the inner search for truth in the inner space of self. Now revealed not in the grand histrionic gesture but in smaller ways. As Yeats put it: when modern people are deeply moved, they look silently into the fireplace.

Stanislavski, living at the intersection of the political and emotional movements towards the significance of self, intuited the necessity for a system to help the actor work within the new demands of the theatre of realism. Nowhere has Stanislavski's influence been more significant than in the United States. In simple historical terms, the Moscow Art Theatre visited America in 1923 and Richard Boleslavsky and Maria Ouspenskya remained in New York to teach their understanding of Stanislavski's system. This led to the adoption of elements of the system by the Group Theater in the 1930s, and ultimately to the founding of the New York Actors' Studio, and the evolution of the Method as taught there by Lee Strasberg in the 1950s. Several members of the studio – notably Marlon Brando, Paul Newman, Rod Steiger, Julie Harris and Geraldine Page – became internationally famous screen actors and lent dynamic to the spread of Method techniques. Stanislavski's first book, *An Actor Prepares*,[6] was published in translation in the US and became almost a Bible of the acting profession there.

The fervent adoption of the Stanislavski system in the United States was more than just an historical coincidence, it was a function of its strong appeal to certain perceptions and needs within the American persona. One of the great American traditions is that the expatriate Whig gentry who founded the republic did it in the name of the common man. The Group Theater of the 1930s, which adopted Stanislavski's system, was politically revolutionary and devoted to the ultimate triumph of the freedom of the individual, or common man, under the aegis of that great post-Jeffersonian, Karl Marx. Emotionally committed to anti-authoritarianism and the freedom of the individual; socially and economically based upon the right to self-improvement, the American sensibility was essentially fertile ground for any philosophy or system geared to the examination and free expression of the soul or psyche of the common man. Thus Stanislavski's focus upon the actor's inner process joined hands with Freud's analysis of the individual psyche and Marx's ultimate triumph of the proletariat, to create a methodology which was ideally suited to the early twentieth-century climate of the American theatre, just beginning as it was, to achieve a self-definition and mirror the flowering of the American social persona, as the common man was coming into his economic (somewhat delayed by the Depression) and political birthright.

More than this. The Method, as parlayed by Lee Strasberg, in conjunction with the burgeoning of a specifically American realistic drama, through the agency of O'Neill, Williams, Miller, etc., gave a unique definition to the American theatre, and worldwide recognition of its achievements. Finally, almost two hundred years after the American Revolution, the American theatre had asserted its independence from Europe. And it had done it in a way consistent with the romantic tradition of that revolution: through feeling, not form, and individuality, not social rules.

The freedom from European autocracy, structure and externalities also meant freedom from trammelling technique. The individual is important and what is interesting about the individual is the unique expression of his or her feelings. And these must be expressed in an individual way, not forced into any technical, physical or vocal form. All that was necessary to the actor was the ability to express his or her feelings at the appropriate time: inner process. And this is the aspect of the Stanislavski system that the Strasberg Method picked up on and turned into a complete process for the actor. Be yourself. You don't need to speak in the well-modulated tones of the European-trained actor – this would not be 'honest' if it is not your own voice; and in any case it is not the way 'real' people speak. You don't have to alter your physical manner through any kind of exercises, you simply had to be able to let your feelings come through in an unmediated way. The Method became a street vernacular for the purpose of playing the man in the street. To take it to the nth degree, it was very egalitarian, another plus in terms of American perceptions: if all you had to do to act was to be yourself then, presumably, anyone could act!

There are, again, a couple of historical reasons why what was in fact a small part of Stanislavski's system was taken over by the Method. Richard Boleslavsky who first taught the system in the United States was only familiar with Stanislavski's early work on 'emotional theory' and inner process. This was compounded by the fact that Stanislavski's later works, *Building a Character*[7] and *Creating a Role*,[8] were not published in the US until long after *An Actor Prepares*; by which time an unbalanced emphasis towards emotional rather than physical techniques had taken hold. But, historical quirks aside, the major reason why only certain elements of Stanislavski's work were adopted in the United States and turned into the Method, was that they fitted certain needs of both American self-perception and the energies of the American theatre at a particular time.

As realism propagated the idea that theatre should minutely recapitulate the details of everyday existence; a 'slice of life' as

lived by the man in the street, free from all restraints or conventions, so it came to be understood that the actor, too, must be
free from any technical restraints, and from limitations upon his
or her freedom of action, or acting. Now, the only way in which
an actor could respond freely, and therefore honestly, was to do
whatever the dictates of his or her emotional feeling produced at
any particular moment. The argument ran: if I am to be 'real',
to play freely and honestly, what have I to draw on but my own
experience, my emotional memories, my particular storehouse of
human responses? Any mediation in this process was seen as some
kind of external imposition, an artificial mask and thus dishonest,
technical trickery.

This was not what Stanislavski had in mind when calling for a
greater concern with inner process, but it was splendidly consonant
with the idea that the concerns of the individual in society are
primary, and what is most real and interesting about the individual
is his or her personal feelings. Thus, the feeling of the moment
became the touchstone of theatrical truth: the self of the actor and
the self of the character were perceived to have a one-to-one
relationship.

In the context of the Method, this led to an emphasis upon
emotion memory, and such other techniques as the 'private
moment', substitution, and the creation of biographies for characters. Emotion memory taught actors to stimulate emotion in the
present by recreating in their imagination the circumstances of a
past event in which an analogous feeling had arisen. The private
moment encouraged actors to examine and reveal the feelings
arising from their own personal emotional problems. Substitution
was a technique whereby an actor substituted the image of someone of their own acquaintance for the actor playing opposite them,
if that acquaintance could produce a stronger emotional response.
Biography was the creation of the life of a character before and
beyond the life given to that character by the author.

It can be seen that all these techniques tend to operate at a
remove from the action of the moment as demanded of a character
by the play; and there is an implicit assumption that the character
is the 'real' person, not a *dramatis persona*, i.e. a mask created to
serve the dramatic purposes of the play's action. Emotion memory
is essentially second-hand. It uses emotion that is stimulated by
a circumstance other than that of the play's immediate action. It

introduces an emotional *non sequitur* into a performance. It can produce irrelevance – the actor is involved with a past situation of his or her own, rather than responding to the action of the present – and thus may transmute the part into the structure of the actor's own, possibly different, emotional needs and dynamics.

Substitution, by definition, takes the actor out of connection with the immediate experience of the play's action. The creation of biographies can weigh the actor down with all manner of irrelevancies and lead to spending performance time filling out the 'life' of the character rather than energetically pursuing the character's action as given in the script. As the quip runs, 'Did Hamlet have an affair with his mother?' 'Only in the touring company.'

So, what we have tended to get in the pursuit of realism through a naturalistic acting process are two confusions. The first between the actor's and the character's emotional and psychological makeup – if the actors aren't playing their own emotional responses then they are perceived as dishonest. The second between the fact of the character as an artefact within a play, both aesthetic constructs, and the character perceived as a 'real' person. This confusion could lead a distinguished actor to say, 'I couldn't play Othello. I wouldn't have killed Desdemona.' Yes, the actor experiences an emotion with which he *supports* the character. Yes, the emotion is in one sense his; but *he* is not jealous or miserly; he is Othello or Harpagon. And, as Bernard Shaw has put it, 'There ain't no such person as Lady Macbeth', in response to the redundant 'realistic' question of how many children did Lady Macbeth have. What is ignored by naturalistic processes such as the Method is the fact that the character is a figment of the playwright's imagination, and has very particular actions to perform within the structure of the play as a whole.

We have noted that there was a qualitative change in the concept and consciousness of self at this time, and self-enquiry can certainly become part of the playwright's concept of character. But the character is still a construct meant to serve the play's action and not the feeling of the actor. The missing element of the individualistic process was precisely the larger circumstance of the play's action: the fact that a playwright creates a logical consistency between the wishes, wants, needs and emotional responses of the character, and the inventions and events of the play's action in which the character is integrally involved. Yes the actor supports action with feeling, but it is a feeling appropriate to the way in which his or her character reacts to the demands of the play's action, and is channelled in such a way both to fulfil that demand and make the most exciting impact on the audience.

The basis of acting isn't personal feeling. Anyone can feel. As Robert Lewis, distinguished teacher and director of the naturalistic process, whose book, *Method or Madness*,[9] was the first to query tenets of the Method, has said: 'If being able to cry is a criterion of good acting, then my Aunt Minnie would have been Duse.' It is being able to fulfil the total demands of a role. With Shakespeare, for example, this obviously means encompassing the poetry. This has been emphasized by Vanessa Redgrave in saying that 'Shakespeare has found some marvellous words to convey things that are far more precise than a great splurge of emotion can convey.'[10] But even in a 'realistic' play, Willie Loman isn't simply 'the guy next door'; he is Miller's iconic salesman encompassing the existential essence of what it means to live and die working within the capitalistic system of America in the mid-twentieth century.

Such Method techniques as emotion memory, private moment and substitution can be useful studio exercises to help the actor explore and tune up his or her instrument; or part of a rehearsal process to explore the range of an actor's response; but the final acting choice must be in the play's terms, not that of the actor's ego. To quote Yeats again:

The heart well worn upon the sleeve
May be the best of sights,
But never, never dangling leave
The liver and the lights.

In certain circumstances, when the dynamics of a role and the psychological makeup of an actor are closely aligned, the technique of pure self-revelation can produce bravura performances, powerful acts of self-display. And it is still alive today, especially in the realm of film where it can produce what has been called by director Oliver Stone 'Ball-istic' acting: a primal, rebellious exhibition of the actor's troubled psyche which enters the space beyond the 'petty book-keeping of ordinary existence'. It is carnivorously individualistic, subject neither to the restraints of ensemble nor to the shape of any part previously written. It is best compared to the old line of actor-managers who probably died with Donald Wolfit, of whom the story is told that a replacement was sent for to play Bassanio to Wolfit's Shylock. The young actor arrived, knocked on the manager's door and said, 'Sir, can you tell me how you want me to play our scenes?' To which the great man replied, 'Oh, don't worry, just stand by the back flat and when I want you I'll come and get you.'

The 'reality' of a performance has no inherent connection with the degree of fidelity with which it reproduces the facts of actual life. Naturalistic detail has no theatrical impact unless it can be employed to build a larger statement than the trivial surface seems to admit. If the voice of the actor is limited to the reporting of the sounds we use for conversation, and the body is geared to the repertoire of sitting, standing, walking, there is the same potential for expression as takes place in life over a cup of tea or coffee. The projection of life must be magnified to suit the optics of theatre, not muted to reveal the subtext of reality.

Frank Wedekind in his 'The art of acting' has suggested that the naturalistic style of acting took on and dies hard because it is easy: 'The actor stuck his hands in his pockets, stood with his back to the audience and waited with the greatest of ease for the next word to be called out to him.'[11] And ease of playing and recognition is still one of its great attractions. Today, aggressive emotional display, larded with 'bad' language, dealing with some topic concerning whatever society perceives to be the current oppressed class, is thought to be 'real' and honest acting work. It is not. It is vulgar, both in the original sense of the word, and vulgar in the sense the words have taken: in the transient, superficial gesture it makes to the illusion of dealing with serious problems. It allows the audience to get away with a shallow ephemeral feeling of relating to 'real' issues – through the meretricious simplicity of the sentimental surface gesture. Actor and audience enjoy a warm and runny feeling without serious effort or experience beyond the self-congratulatory one of the shared moment. Such acting is based upon the false premise that display of feeling is of supreme importance. It leads to momentary ego gratification such as can be found in the rock-and-roll posturings of the MTV sensibility: and lo and behold, Madonna now acts!

Charles Marowitz, one of the earliest proponents of the Method has said: 'Any theory that persuades me that sincerity of feeling

and truthfulness of action are all that is required in the creation
of art misunderstands aesthetics as much as it overprizes individuality.'[12] To largeness of feeling must be added selectivity and strin-
gency: a discipline of detachment.

Forms of common or 'natural' behaviour tend to obscure rather
than reveal truth. As Peter Hall has said, one of the problems
with naturalism is that it shows us more than we need to know.
The presented dramatic reality is always some form of ideal construct, selected and shaped in a particular way. Powerful acting
is both human and transcendental; conveying a sense of dealing
with overarching values, and those perspectives which not so much
individuate humanity but make it what it is *sub specie aeternitatis*.
Immediate recognizability can be seductive and give credence to
the idea that if it fools you into thinking it was 'real', it must be
good. There is the story of the man coming out of a performance
of *Death of a Salesman* and telling his companion: 'That damned
New England territory never was any good.' It goes back to the
phenomenological problem we discussed earlier. The feeling we
have that a character in a play is real, and therefore adaptable to
other relationships and could sit down with us at dinner, is 'an
illusion born of his or her resemblance to a human being' such as
ourselves. It is not a prime criterion of acting.

The self-defeating end of the criterion of reality as a judgement
of acting is, finally, that it is not possible to have an art of the
actor, seen as a presence, if his or her virtuosity simply consists
of disappearing into the 'reality' of the phenomenological environment.

Chapter 6

The dynamics of acting: skills

If, then, the apparent representation of reality, lifelikeness, is not a sufficient or necessary criterion for the judgement of acting, can we point to anything that gives us a basis for discriminating between acting we would call good and bad? What we come back to is the basic element of theatre, the actor's body as fundamental presence and sign. Although, as we have already suggested, there can be no absolutely precise vocabulary of signs, it is the sign the audience sees; the skill with which an actor creates that sign will have a significant effect upon the audience's experience of the theatrical event. The more skilfully the actor makes the sign, the more likelihood is there that the audience will experience it as the actor intended. So it is not lifelikeness, it is not feeling or engendering of emotion *per se*, but skill (in creating the sign) that seems to be a basic way of approaching the actor's craft.

What does this skill consist of? We have already spoken of the importance of balance and the idea of the actor's centre. Because we apprehend with our senses, mainly our eyes, we tend to think of ourself as located in our heads. This is a particular problem for the actor because we do read the script and think about it with our heads. But we act with our bodies, and respond from our centre where physical balance, breath and nervous impulses come together. From this centre we allow the impulses to flow outward and inform all other parts of our body in such a way that a powerful communicative sign will be made. This impulse, through the actor's exercise of skills, is channelled, controlled and focused. The impulse cannot have a simply arbitrary outward expression or the actor will be one who will 'unpack [your] heart with words, and fall a-cursing like a very drab.'[1] The sign 'in the very tempest, torrent . . . [and] whirlwind of passion must acquire and beget a temperance'.[2]

The 'temperance', the focus and control are a function of the skill with which an actor creates a sign; usually by the use of gestures: the doing of some physical activity, including speaking. The right gesture will be the precise, integrated centre of everything taking place on stage at that moment. It will have an inevitability in the way in which it illustrates the essence of the moment of action as intuited by the playwright. It is calculated, but appears effortless – yet another of the dichotomies of theatre. It will be the right choice, at the right moment, with the right dynamics. It will be articulated so as to command attention, while integrated to appear to have arisen unconsciously from the character's needs: a perfect balance of life and art.

The gesture arises from the action of the moment, catalysed by the impulse to respond in the actor. It arises from the actor's centre, seat of balance, and emotional force. It embraces and focuses the powerful need of the moment and communicates this to the audience. And the right gesture never does more than is necessary. Good actors are aware of the space and time within which they are working and just how strong an impression they need to make on it. The gesture will be taken as far as the space and time requires, but no farther. Less good actors are not good judges of this felt theatrical pulse and will tend to do more than is required, to overfill the moment. Equally less good actors may not fill the moment strongly enough, there will be a tentative quality about the gesture, and it will lack the power of a clear outline, it will be fuzzy, uncertain, and fail to grab the audience's attention in the necessary way. Tentative actors who do not fill their gestures tend to have a blurred outline, or to be working behind a scrim. The effect is as with a bottle of liquid which is not quite full: when it is shaken up, i.e. responds to an impulse, it is frothy and has a carbonated effect that blurs the outline. When completely full, it has a hard, clear outline no matter what position it is held in.

The full clear gesture is both connected (emanates from the centre of power) and controlled. Just as a bridle on a horse makes its reactions stronger and more immediate, so the theatre, which deals in powerful emotions, needs discipline, and by restraint increases the power of the spontaneous. Not only is the gesture filled and controlled, but economy is exercised in its use. Chekhov has said that when a man spends the least possible number of movements over some definite action, that is grace. Stanislavski said that generality is the enemy of art. Shakespeare tells his actors, 'do not saw the air too much with your hand'.[3] The old actor's advice is 'Do less!' Do not let the overuse of trammelling day-by-day detail obscure the audience's focus upon the larger processes of life: do not obscure the wood with the trees.

Overillustration is probably one of the giveaways of the untrained or amateur actor: one has to feel like one is acting, something has to be going on! And of course, if one is spending all one's time acting, then the playing of the necessary actions of your character will be lost beneath the whirligigs of your enthusiastic self. An actor who seems to be doing very little, yet is always the focus of the audience's attention, is probably acting well. Presuming that actions are connected to the impulse and derive from the actor's centre of power, then clarity and stillness will tend to mean strength and give presence; busyness weakens. A very simplistic but concrete illustration of the point is the actor who fidgets or shuffles. When an actor has reached the end of a movement, the image he or she presents should be absolutely still and clear, like a full stop at the end of a sentence. It is like, to go back to athletics, the manner in which a gymnast lands at the end of some improbable feat: absolute stillness is the ideal, gains the most marks and makes the greatest impression. This shows control, balance and complete confidence in the power of the image being presented to the audience.

Stillness is also connected to energy. With clarity there is no waste. A still body frames itself with space and intensifies the moment, giving it the necessary heightened impact required by the stage. And, in a sense, it is getting the effect for free. The actor is not overdoing, dissipating energy, working too hard. The impact is created by filling more and doing less. Focus and concentration achieve the effect, while the actor is husbanding energy against the time when the play requires it to be expended.

For the skilled actor, physical discipline and control are givens not ends. They are part of the relaxed yet clear and strong outline of the actor's physical presence on stage. They do not limit the actor, they simply provide a strong dynamic base from which the many different tasks of the role may be played. The aim of the actor is to make the obviously right gesture surprising, without losing its necessary effect. The ability to achieve variety while maintaining clarity is one touchstone of acting. One of the demands placed upon the professional is the ability to make constant adjustments and discover new choices without changing the truth of the action or nature of the character. The amateur probably clings thankfully to the first choice that seems to work. The need for subtle variety is never greater than in much realistic drama where a lot of sitting around and talking goes on. The ability to illustrate this simple activity in four or five different ways while still retaining the dynamics of relationship adds texture and interest to the *mise-en-scène*.

We probably all have our favourite acting moments. One that sticks with me is a fairly simple illustration of the giving of variety to an everyday activity. In a production of *Treasure Island*, one of the pirate characters asked for an apple. It was tossed to him, and instead of catching it in his hand, he caught it on the point of his knife, then started to peel it. The gesture, done smilingly, showed physical skill, danger, threat and good humour, all in the performance of the simple act of getting an apple to eat. Harold Pinter, in particular among modern playwrights, has a knack of providing everyday activities – drinking a glass of water or passing a salt cellar – which call for the actor to place a frame of stillness around the gesture, thus investing it with a significance, and potential threat, far greater than the banality of the action would presume.

The idea of framing a gesture brings up another important and recognizable skill of the actor, that of timing. Although a necessary skill in all forms of playing, it is most evident in comedy where the success or otherwise of timing gets immediate judgement in whether or not the audience laughs. The handling of verbal repartee is an important skill in comic playing. It may be likened to fencing with the tongue. The actor must have quick verbal reflexes, and be able to speak distinctly at a swift pace. Lip and tongue agility are necessary skills, as is the ability to use a variety of head tones to be able to point the line. Head tones, because wit tends to be intellectual and derive from the head rather than the actor's emotional base; also head tones, lacking the resonance of lower notes, are sharper and more pointed. An actor must be aware of the shape of a line so that, by use of rhythmical stress, he or she can set up the audience to laugh at the right moment. The actor builds the tension of the line until the audience feels the need of release: poised, breath held expectantly as the actor stresses the crucial point of the line – hence 'pointing' – to let the audience's repressed energy come out in a laugh – *à la* Freud.

There is a complementary skill in playing the laugh once the actor has got it. The audience must be allowed to have its laugh – that's what it has come for – but it can't be allowed to hold back the necessarily swift pace of the performance for too long. The actor must have very fast verbal brakes. He or she must expect the laugh, but not anticipate it, take the line full tilt, then hold for the audience to enjoy itself and appreciate the actor's skill, then accelerate away just as the laugh begins to fade, thus quelling the audience and making them listen for the next laugh. The ability to play with the audience is a necessary skill of comedic acting: knowing just how to play the audience with a line – rather like a fisherman with a line. Actors will talk of 'laying a line out', 'gathering it in', 'making the audience wait' to heighten the expectation, 'losing a laugh'. One of the dangers of playing comedy is that the actor will begin to play last night's performance, with the rhythms and stresses that were successful then: playing for the laugh, rather than playing the action and the line in the present with an ear on how tonight's audience is responding. The response can also be mysterious. Donald Sinden tells of playing Malvolio whereby if he crossed his legs one way on a line he would get a laugh, if he crossed his legs the other way he wouldn't! The skill in being able to discover this, then play the lines and the audience freshly every night is one the actor must develop. It must be said that timing, in its highest reaches of perfection, timing, like Sinden's crossed legs, tends to be something of a mystery, a gift from the gods.

Donald Sinden also tells of having problems in developing a character while playing farce. He consulted Edith Evans who said, 'Of course, you see in farce you don't have a play to help you.' Farce doesn't depend upon verbal skills; it is essentially physical. Finding as many ways as possible for the character to run into or trip over situations. Physical timing, together with balance (again) and physical imagination, becomes a prime skill. To make a simple distinction between the comedian and the farceur: if there are stairs or steps on the stage, the audience may expect, at some time in the play, the farceur to fall down them; the comedian however will move swiftly and gracefully down them, maybe pausing to launch a *bon mot*. The tragedian, of course, will pause four-square at the top.

The skill of physical timing extends beyond comedy into all forms of dramatic presentation. It is, in fact, a way in which all actors will phrase or punctuate a line. Whether it be the raising of the arms to the heavens to make the body an exclamation mark on such a line as 'Oh, ye Gods!' or the simple placing of a cup with small sound into its saucer to affirm a stop at the end of a line. The use of physical gesture and properties to point and punctuate lines is a skill which all actors must acquire to clarify, heighten and physically reveal – activity commands more attention than speech – the action intended by a line. The need physically to express the intention of a line is displayed even at a first reading when actors use the turning of a page of script to punctuate their readings and to express the energy they feel from the intention of its lines.

Control, connection, economy, variety, filling, timing, pointing: these are all necessary skills of the actor which enable him or her to create and communicate the shape of the appropriate gesture to the audience. This will achieve the most direct, vivid and interesting response in the audience, consistent with the necessary dynamics of the particular moment of action it is intended to illustrate. The audience recognizes feeling within itself; it does not necessarily recognize feeling within the actor. Even tears are not reliable; some actors can engender these by secreting onion in their hands, or looking directly into the hot spot of the lights – both techniques if not skills! But an audience can recognize skill. Once a person is aware of the skills that are operating on the stage, a performance may be watched with what might be termed a bifocalism. This is the audience equivalent of what we have termed the actor's controlled schizophrenia or doubleness. Not by a conscious suspension of belief, but by an awareness of how an effect is being made, an audience member can both experience and appreciate the effect at the same time. Possibly some marginal experience of the emotional moment is lost by the intellectual withholding of some empathy, but this is at least compensated for by the extra experience of the conscious art of the moment and the appreciation of the actor's skill. Knowing how difficult it is to

make something seem easy, to be able to perceive the art that is
employed to disguise art, is one of the sophisticated pleasures of
the appreciation of acting.

Chapter 7

The dynamics of acting: process

Skills are the specific, recognizable part of an actor's work made evident in performance. Before there are skills, there is process. Process is the way in which an actor goes about discovering what it is performance skills should be applied to. There is no one process and, indeed, finding the right process for the right circumstance is itself a skill. Most actors work eclectically, using whatever elements of process seem to have worked for them over the years. But probably the most fundamental and commonly acknowledged, if not agreed upon, basic process is that of Stanislavski.

Leaving aside the controversial concept of emotion memory, already discussed, there are some basic principles of the Stanislavski system which are generally accepted, if not universally adopted, as a valid process for the actor's work on, at least, realistic texts. The process requires actors to approach a text by breaking it down into units of action, or 'beats'. There is a probably apocryphal story that it was originally little 'bits', but the Russian accent made it sound like 'beats' to the western ear! So beats we have; which does in fact lend an appropriately active and rhythmical sound to the process. Beats are units of textual time which have a consistent preoccupation with a specific action on the part of the characters: a period of time when characters don't change their objectives or tactics. The individual units fit consistently together to create the main action of the play.

We have just mentioned the character's objective. This is another part of the system. It is what the characters want, what their actions are geared to achieve, what they step on stage to get. The objective is complemented by the concept of the obstacle (whatever stands in the way of the characters getting what they

want) and of tactics (how characters either change their objective
in a small way, or go about getting around obstacles). The interplay of all the characters' objectives creates the super-objective,
the overarching want, sometimes called the 'spine' of the character.

What a character says that he or she wants may not be the
same as what, indeed, they *do* want. This is where the concept of
subtext becomes a part of Stanislavski's system. It is the character's actual intention or meaning which may underlie a statement.
When a character says, 'I think you asked a really insightful
question in class, and would like to discuss it further with you',
the character may actually mean, 'I think you have got a really
great body and would like to get to know you better.' An actor
needs to know a character's actual intention to be able to play it
validly. Of course, if a character actually reveals the hidden subtext, it is what we would call a Freudian slip, which shows the
close relationship of the concept of subtext to the principles of
psychology, and Stanislavski's concern with inner action.

The 'if', another part of Stanislavski's system, enables the actor
to make appropriate choices of action by putting him- or herself
into the character's situation. 'What, given that I am Macbeth,
Stanley Kowalski, Millamant, would *I* do if *I* were in this situation?' The concept of the character's textual situation is crucial
here, as it implies consideration of all the given circumstances of
the text. It was the truncating of this concept into 'What would
I do if I were in this situation?' that led to one of the major
problems with the Method: the abuse of emotion memory and the
solipsism of playing oneself.

Given circumstances. This last link in the chain refers to the
details of character and situation that enable actors to give a
particular shape to their characters' actions. Stanley Kowalski in
A Streetcar Named Desire, and Horner in *The Countrywife* are great
'studs' of their time. But, because their time is quite different, so
will be the manner in which they play their actions. Again, this
was a part of Stanislavski's system which tended to be ignored by
Method adherents. Circumstances such as climate, dialect, physical type, age and occupation may distinguish certain personal
attributes of character, but they are not necessarily sufficient for
the actor to place the character validly within the total demands
of the text. Theatrical conventions within the play, the structure
of the language, the social manner of the time, are all a part of

the given circumstances with which an actor has to deal, and of the process by which, as we shall see later, the actor comes to terms with the style of the play.

Stanislavski's system is important as a template of acting process, because it was the first and got an awful lot right. What it most conspicuously did was to help an actor look at a text as a map to action. For Stanislavski, the actor's process was based upon a careful understanding and analysis of the text to gain a clear sense of the total action of the play – an advance in itself over the received principle whereby actors simply concerned themselves with their own parts – and how the character's needs and wants both fed into and were a response to this. The actor would also gather all the information the text gave about the nature – bodily, circumstantial and emotional – of his or her character, to create a physical and psychological profile of the character; even, possibly, creating a biography of what the character's background may have been before the events of the play. This information is put together with the character's wants to discover the psychological responses within the actor/character: how the character would feel and therefore react within the situation. The process is textual analysis to circumstances, to feeling in response to those circumstances, which becomes the catalyst to action.

That it is an overly analytical process is a function of the scientific mind-set of the time. That it tended to confuse, in its desire to ensure that a character had an inner as well as outer life, the truth of life with the truth of art, is an understandable overstatement of a romantic concern to make the point. That part of the process was taken out of context and turned into actor ego gratification was not Stanislavski's fault.

As Stanislavski developed and refined his system he moved away from the conception of acting as the exploration and revelation of the character's inner psychological process, towards the more concrete idea of the playing of physical actions: a move from feeling back towards physical sign. The principle here being that any action directed towards the achievement of a desire or want will generate spontaneous supporting feeling: do the act and the feeling will follow. This is not a return towards 'external' acting but the recognition of the Gestalt nature of the human psychophysiology: mind and body are interrelated not separate entities (a final break with the neoclassical Cartesian sensibility), and the body's feelings are stored in muscle memory.

Many of the valid processes which an actor may be exposed to and use to create his or her own process are, today, derived from this later physical concept of Stanislavski. This concept provides a bridge from purely naturalistic acting process – concentration on inner process and subsuming the part within the actor's own persona – to the broader theatricalized tradition of creating a score of physical actions and presenting this to the audience.[1]

Three of Stanislavski's disciples, Eugene Vakhtangov, Vsevold Meyerhold and Michael Chekhov, continued the movement towards a more physically based process, with Chekhov evolving his technique of the psychological gesture, which exemplified the concept of physical gesture embodying psychological response. The process asks the actor to work with what he or she determines as the basic qualities of the character. Then, by a combination of empirical experience and imagination, the actor works on the physical expression of this quality until some gesture is discovered that produces a strong emotional reaction in the actor. The gesture must be simple, strong and clear, and once found it is repeated forcefully until the most powerful supporting feeling of the quality is present. Once the psychology of the character has been penetrated and physically outlined – a physical spine has been created with roots in an emotional base – it may be refined and given more subtlety and sophistication by further experimentation with detail, as required by the given circumstances. What this process gives the actor is a solid, tangible physical base. The psychological gesture is like a charcoal sketch of a character, done broadly and simply with the least possible number of strokes to produce the strongest effect.

Fundamental to all creativity is the concept that every act of creation starts from some kind of impulse. The impulse may be an idea; it may be an image; it may spring from pure imagination; or, as is usually the case with theatre, it will be the actor's response to a play text. The first impulse is usually a direct expression of instinctive response, but it is often the case that too much intellectualism, too much analysis, tends to lead the actor to censor that response: it is thought too 'impulsive', too strange, or not imaginative or unique enough. It is here that a focus upon a physical process of response to text helps the actor to accept and go with the initial impulse and be open to all its possibilities.

The impulse is an instinctive movement towards action. It becomes conscious when the actor's mind becomes aware of what the body wants to do: the body having checked over the experiential litany of responses to the impulse that it has stored away. The actor can accept and go with the body's impulsive/instinctive choice or can check over the litany in the mind and select another choice of action.

This action is played in the form of an activity which expresses the impulse. Usually the activity affects another actor, i.e. is an impulse for that actor to respond by playing an action. In this way, action moves back and forth in response to impulses and in the form of activities, and a scene is created.

The purpose of the action is to effect some change. This will be the actor's objective in the scene: to effect change in the relationship with the other actors in the scene – to win approval; get a kiss; cause the death; or more simply, share a cup of tea.

The circumstances of the situation will condition the way in which the action is played. What we call, after Stanislavski, the 'given circumstances' are the rules of the game of theatre that actors are involved in playing. The rules are contained within the script and must be understood and agreed upon by the players so that their creative impulses will take the shape appropriate to the game. To draw an analogy with athletic games again, the impulse to make a winning shot will be communicated through the racket in tennis and the feet in soccer; not the other way around. The given circumstances also distinguish one theatrical game, event or, simply, production from another; as we shall see, they also form the basis for the creation of style. Given circumstances determine the choice, shape and playing of the action; they also determine the sensibility and form of the event.

Guided by the given circumstances, the actor's basic process is then to make physical choices that communicate the intention of the impulses gained from the script or text. The interrelationship of all the choices of all actors creates a 'score' of actions which is the performance. Once discovered in rehearsal, and agreed upon by the players, the score remains a constant. However, the way in which the score is played will vary somewhat at each performance, as the actors respond to the immediate rhythm of the occasion flowing from fellow actors and from the audience. It is this margin of flexibility in playing that keeps the vitality in performance.

The play factor stimulates renewed vitality in performance; allows for spontaneity within fixed structures; permits the 'God to come'. Playing encourages the release of instinctive impulses: that flow of energy which stems from the basic process of creation and which underlies the rhythm upon which the actor rides, from the first impulse, through the creation of the score of actions, into performance.

Playing is closely connected to a crucial but less tangible element of the actor's creative process: imagination. We are back to Plato's 'Divine Madness', not subject to reason, definition . . . or discourse! Imagination is the kind of active dreaming that informs children's play, changing experience into flexible, free-flowing images, releasing the mind from the domination of 'reality' and making poetry out of the everyday stuff of life. The realm of the imagination makes the actor a poet. It has been said that the poet sees more than most people, and records more than they see. So with the actor, who absorbs more, and communicates more. Imagination is the catalyst that sets the playful reaction going, taps into the wellsprings of our communal store of possible dreams and human memories, expanding the boundaries of normal reactions to produce the extraordinary. So the instrument is played in some unsuspected way while still maintaining the necessary effect. And playing begets playing to expand the bounds of the possible available to the actor.

It was Rudolf Laban who, in the mid-twentieth century, converted the process of imaginative playing into a system, and concretely related it to the development of character.[2] This system was based upon the principle that action is the physical form or pattern of an effort made to change a given circumstance. Effort can be perceived and measured in its various components:

- the time of an action – this can vary from quick to sustained;
- the weight of an action – this can vary from light to strong;
- the direction of an action – this can vary from direct to indirect.

These factors may all be permutated, and combinations of them will produce what Laban called the 'Basic Action Drive' of a character. This is similar to what Stanislavski would call the through-line or spine of character; but in Laban's system it is an essentially physical construct which is both highly concrete and capable of flexibility: it may be adjusted along a spectrum of effort that will range from assertive/contending to indulgent/yielding.

Having received basic impulses from the rhythm that his or her character projects from the text, the actor plays with the Action Drive system to discover where the character lies along its spectrum. For example, if the character's effort is discovered to be direct, strong and sustained, the character is what Laban called a *Presser*. If direct, strong, and quick, a *Puncher*. At the other end of the spectrum, a direct, light and sustained effort makes the character a *Glider*. The system has great flexibility in that all the effort factors may be permutated and adjusted by the actor as further discoveries are made about the character in rehearsal. What it does, is to give the actor a strong yet flexible physical base for the character in the rehearsal process.

The system presumes that emotional memory is embedded in muscle memory: the senses collect experience as we go through life, and these are absorbed into the body and stored away waiting for impulses to re-energize them. The actor, having determined the Basic Action Drive of the character, then only has to play the action given by the text for the emotional support to be engendered. The actor does not have to focus upon trying to recall feeling; the focus is upon playing the action as conditioned by the given circumstances, and the emotional response will 'respond'.

This system is particularly useful in non-realistic styles of theatre, but is equally applicable to character development in forms of realism. Once the Basic Action Drive is discovered, the character may be taken into various everyday activities – washing dishes, typing, changing a tyre – to discover its rhythms and responses in these situations. Permutations can be explored. A character that is basically a Puncher may, in a given situation, make an adjustment to one of the effort factors as a tactical way of dealing with the situation. For example, a Puncher who wants the last seat on an air flight in a high-demand situation may decide to change the weight of his or her movement, to yield somewhat, which will change the assertiveness of the gestures; to knock gently upon the reception desk rather than to bang forcefully. Putting this the other way around, if a Puncher lessens the weight of gesture at any time, it will bring a yielding response emotionally; all movement reveals some feature of inner life.

Actors can explore numerous situations where a change of the weight/time/direction factor produces tactical adjustments of the character's approach. Such changes can be especially useful in discovering the smaller character mannerisms that can etch in detail and fill out the broader physical qualities: how a character holds a cigarette, pours a drink, bites fingernails, etc.

Laban's system is in many ways derived from, and an elaboration of, what Stanislavski called Tempo-Rhythm. Indeed, one of the ironies of the contemporary approaches to acting process is that Stanislavski, owing to somewhat invalid association with Strasberg's Method, is all too often regarded simplistically as propounding a system limited to the generating of internal, psychological response in the actor and relying upon emotion as the basis of the actor's work. As has been suggested, one of the reasons for this was the historical accident that there was a twelve-year gap between the publication in English of the first part of his System (*An Actor Prepares*) and the second part (*Building a Character*). Stanislavski's intention was that what was perceived in the English-speaking theatre as two separate approaches should in fact be one integrated system. A literal translation of his work in Russian would be: An Actor's Work on Himself, (1) inner process and (2) *vploščenie*, or 'incarnation'. By the latter term, Stanislavski meant the process by which the actor's imaginative impulse is given concrete form shaped by the actor's physical skills. Stanislavski's intention was an integrated psychophysical process. In this, the purpose of inner process was to tune the actor's sensitivity, imagination and emotional range so that it would expand, feed and support the playing of physical actions. These were the signs by which the actor communicated with the audience, and which Stanislavski clearly believed to be the end product of the actor's process.

Stanislavski had a strong sense of the importance of play to the acting process, and introduced improvisation as a rehearsal tool. Charles Marowitz tells an instructive story of Stanislavski being unable to get the right sense of a childlike quality from one of his actors. He invited the actor to his house to 'talk it over'. When the actor arrived, Stanislavski was seated on the floor in the midst of a pile of toys. Warily, the actor sat down and began to humour

Stanislavski by playing with the toys. After a while a genuine fascination took over and the two men became engrossed in play, whereupon Stanislavski gleefully said, 'There, now you have it. That's what your character is like.'[3]

The use of games and improvisations is a fundamental part of the training process of most actors today, and it has become increasingly a part of the rehearsal process. Playscripts can be seen as a structure of human games, based upon the learned experience we all have stored within us. By confronting the action physically, an actor can release the body's spontaneous response to the nature of the game. Through the physicality of the game, the emotional content of the action can also be released. Searching for inner feeling through intellectual understanding can often produce a self-involved and static result. Attacking a role physically can break down inhibitions, release energy and reveal the parameters of the action.

To take one of the classics of the naturalistic theatre, *The Cherry Orchard*, there is a scene at the end of Act III in which Lopahin reveals that he has bought the estate, finally crushing any hopes Madame Ranevskya might have had of saving it, and meaning that she must leave her family home forever. Chekhov's direction is that Madame Ranevskya is 'collapsed, weeping bitterly'. What is actually happening is that her past and present are being destroyed. To help the actress gain a strong sense of this action, an improvisation could be played in which Lopahin can actually go around the rehearsal set breaking it up – overturning furniture, throwing out ornaments, etc. – while Ranevskya follows him trying to save it, put it back together. This activity could give the actor a very strong sense of her subtext and emotional state. Lopahin too, could gain from the exercise for, although his action is not vicious or bent on deliberate destruction, the turning over of the room will give him a physical focus for getting out the drunken euphoria he is feeling. After such an improvisation, both actors can return to the text with a much stronger purchase on the action.

A robust game such as the above can help an actor to get at deeply rooted subtext in naturalistic plays. Verse plays often present a different problem, where the densely poetic language can trap an actor into surface delivery of rhetorical values. Here again, a physical approach to the text within a game structure can help the actor to discover a scene is not about verse or poetic imagery, but about action. There are a couple of scenes in *Othello* (Act III, Scene iii and Act IV, Scene i) in which Iago is tempting Othello, or poisoning him against Cassio and Desdemona. The scenes are subtly different. In the first scene, Iago is more tempting; in the second more goading. Physical images that spring from the nature of the action of the scenes might include an angler playing a fish, a spider enmeshing its victim, or a bullfight. The first scene seems to lend itself to the angling image (this might be reinforced by saying that Iago has Othello 'on a string'). The actors can explore the dynamics of the scene if a rope is tied around Othello and put into the hands of Iago who now, literally, has Othello on a string and can play him like a fish. As he pulls on the rope, plays it out when he meets resistance, discovers when to strike, Iago will experience the physical properties of the lines, and gain a strong sense of the physical relationship in space that the ebb and flow of the scene demands. For his part, Othello will physically experience the pull of Iago's temptation, how strongly he needs to resist, and the way in which he is pulled into Iago's net.

A similar exercise may be done for Act IV, Scene i, using the bullfight metaphor. Rehearsing in a defined space, Iago could have a cape and a stick (with a padded end) with which to goad Othello as the lines suggest. The image of a trapped, maddened bull is also a useful one for Othello in this scene, and will help the actor rise to his full dynamics. Physical exploration in this manner can be used as part of the rehearsal process on any text.

Sometimes it can take the form of a fairly vigorous and sophisticated improvisation, sometimes a simple child's game. There is a scene in *The Importance of Being Earnest* in which Algernon has John Worthing's cigarette case and is refusing to give it back – a chase ensues. Now the scene could be carefully blocked by a director; but it seems to lend itself quite obviously to the children's game of tag. Exploring it this way will not only open up numerous patterns and choices, but keep the playful energy in the scene. After all, in many ways John and Algy are still children and getting at this quality in tension with the clothing mask and gentlemanly manner demanded by their social station could be a useful exercise for the actors.

The game and improvisation approach to process can help actors discover a broader range of possibilities for their character.

Sometimes actors get stuck in a particular set of physical rhythms: it may be their own, a character they have recently played, gimmicks they fall back on when they are unsure of what they are doing, or preconceptions about the part other productions may have given them. Discussion, character analysis and biographies are fine in their way but they may not get beyond intellectual understanding into physical response. Sometimes the discovery of one physical element that 'feels right' can release an actor into a full characterization. Alec Guinness likes to start from how his character walks; Laurence Olivier had a penchant for false noses. Character building is often as much an intuitive leap from a physical impulse which is then developed by plugging into the rhythms of the text, as a carefully thought out set of building blocks balanced one upon the other.

There are probably three basic ways of using improvisation as part of the process of exploring a text. The first is to work through an analogous situation closer to the actor's own experience: to explore the balcony scene in *Romeo and Juliet* by using a doorstep 'goodnight' situation between newly met boy and girl. Second, there is the more physically confrontational or game approach, such as the above examples from *The Cherry Orchard* and *Othello*. A third set of improvisation is to flesh out an actor's sense of both situation and character by playing out circumstances which are outside the textual action but could inform the life of the play. An example would be an improvisation which might be called 'At home with the Brabantios'. In the first act of *Othello*, there is a good deal of reference as to how Othello wooed Desdemona while a guest at Brabantio's house. This all occurs before Shakespeare, classically, begins his play at the point of attack. The circumstance is, however, crucial to the nature of the relationship between Othello, Brabantio and Desdemona. Improvising the at-home situation would enable Othello and Desdemona to explore their relationship before it falls apart – something which isn't developed in the text – and add immediacy to Brabantio's sense of betrayal, and to Desdemona's long speech describing the wooing circumstances.

Any play text is the reduction into words, ciphers and signs on paper of the flesh-and-blood inspirations of the author in his or her creative state. Actors need to discover the organic pulse behind the printed page. This may not happen if actors learn lines by rote and move through spatial patterns which, however sensitively and scrupulously thought out by a director, are still limited to one person's responses. Improvisation not only employs a wider palette of experience, but stimulates the actor's imagination. Further, discoveries made by the actor can be more dynamic than those offered by a director. If the syntax of a production is embedded in games and improvisations, an actor can gain an experience of the demands of the action. The danger of too much intellectualism is a distancing from the physical dynamics of the character: you can intellectually learn to swim on dry land, then drown the minute you touch water. The playing period, stimulating the imagination while learning what works and doesn't, in other words failing safely, is important to the process.

Having said what an important place improvisation now has in the actor's process, it must be allowed that not all actors accept or like the technique. I have been in situations where the director's attempt to use improvisation to explore a text has been dismissed by experienced actors: 'I have been a professional for thirty years and I don't need your kiddies' games!' And in one sense it is perfectly true: the actor knows his or her job or wouldn't have survived. All seasoned actors have discovered their own way of working, and part of this is, of course, a permanent state of improvisation – the way in which the actor modulates between his or her sense of the text and the shape the director is giving: the actors find a way to make that shape their own.

It is said that improvisation never comes to terms with the words, it is a way of avoiding the hard problems of the text. And this can be true – any process can be pursued invalidly. But the more open and willing an actor is to renew and expand his or her process, the more likely is that actor's work to remain vital. A few years ago, John Gielgud in his seventies and distinguished for his voice, when rehearsing Peter Brook's production of Seneca's *Oedipus*, was perfectly willing to 'muck in', physically improvise and make a fool of himself in the secure family of his peers. As all actors must, finally, be willing to do.

In pragmatical terms, the improvisational process is sometimes seen as hopelessly idealistic, that the exigencies of time in professional theatre do not allow for 'extraneous' activity. Certainly in the old weekly rep system, in which actors were performing one play, rehearsing another, and learning a third in any one week (in itself a process which made certain improvisatory demands), actors had very little time to do more than pull a 'line' from their carpetbag, and cigarbox greasepaint stash, and hope to remember the words and moves. Today, the average three- to four-week rehearsal period allows more time for exploration, and games and improvisation can be a useful part of this process.

A further physical technique in an actor's process is the use of masks, both as a training device and as a rehearsal tool. The idea of mask, both as artefact and metaphor has been consistent throughout the history of theatre. Primitive tribes used animal masks both to imitate and propitiate the spirit of the animal they were hunting, their gods, or whatever forces were thought to govern their destinies on earth. The power of the shaman, one of the earliest actors, came through this association. So the idea of control and the assumption of spirit was an early attribute of the mask.

Mask formally enters the tradition of western theatre with the Greeks. Here it not only defines the physiognomy of the character but illustrates its essential emotional response to the action of the drama. Again, not necessarily as a fixed artefact, but as a fixed essence, mask is present in the medieval theatre, somewhat socialized and laicized in form of Deadly Sins, Good Deeds, Vice, etc. This was to make it quite clear to an unsophisticated audience of simple faith what essential function such characters played in the passing pageant of life. Quick recognition of character for an illiterate and naïve audience was also a function of the use of mask by the *Commedia dell'Arte* in the fifteenth to seventeenth centuries.

Mask as artefact, and indeed as metaphor, disappeared in the bourgeois realistic theatre, as display of wealth and concern for the problems of Mammon, rather than Godhead or spirit, took over the theatre. The dissolving of the mask into the 'real' face of the actor continued as bourgeois theatre gave way to that of the common man.

The return to the use of mask was more a function of anthropology than of the theatre. The great archeological period of the late nineteenth century gave us much of our knowledge of the Greek theatre (as well as returning us to Shakespeare's open thrust), and in the context of this there was a return of interest in the mask as a primitive artefact of ritual, worship and improvisation. Jarry, after the Satyr plays, wanted to use masks in his production of *Ubu Roi* (1896); Gordon Craig began to publish *Mask* in 1908; Meyerhold began to use masks in his studio in 1914 and, most significantly, Copeau began to use masks in his explorations of Molière at his École du Vieux Colombier at about the same time.

Apart from the odd gesture by O'Neill and Yeats, masks went out of favour again during the highly naturalistic post-1930s. They made a comeback, particularly in the United States, in the revolutionary 1960s, in the social and political theatre of Peter Schumann and the Bread and Puppet Theatre; Brian Davis in the San Francisco Mime Troupe; and the farmworker-oriented Teatro Campesino under Luis Valdez. All of this, of course, being prefigured by the father (at least) of modern political theatre, Bertolt Brecht, who used masks in his production of *The Caucasian Chalk Circle* in the 1950s.

Masks, then, have been used in theatre that wished to do more than simply deal in face-to-face terms with the problems of everyday persons in everyday situations. They have always been concerned with essences and universal values. They tend to be an icon or, to return to our semiotic language, a sign for something larger than themselves.

With that thought in mind, we must return to Jacques Copeau, who is the catalysing force behind the contemporary use of mask in acting process. Copeau's aim, both in his theatre and his school, was to strip theatre bare of all unnecessary accretions, be they the overinflated gestures of boulevard romanticism, or the too particular small details of naturalism. The stripping included both the actor and the stage. The *tréteau nu* was Copeau's precept, the bare stage (after Shakespeare) upon which actors would create the spatial circumstances required by the text. As for the actor, Copeau wanted one with no preconceptions, who would respond totally to the impulses of the text. The Total Actor's impulse would be discovered physically, not intellectually. Copeau rejected small gestures, stemming from small ideas, manifested in small words, emanating from the face, and having no connection with deeper and more total human response.

Copeau believed the body preceded the mind: *in the beginning was not the word but the body*. In order to get the actor to respond totally with the body, Copeau found he had to take away the face. There is a story that in order to get an actor to relax into her body, he one day threw a handkerchief over her face: the neutral mask was born. The neutral mask is essentially a training tool using what Grotowski was later to call the principle of *via negativa*, the stripping of the actor of all unnecessary personal quirks and the neutralizing of his or her body as an instrument – a *tabula rasa* on which the character may be etched. The neutral mask emphasizes the body and throws into high relief any busy or unnecessary gestures and actions. Actors play with more personal freedom, and with greater physical economy and scale. It is important that during mask exercises actors do not impose upon the mask; they should absorb and let the mask inform the body.

Work in the neutral mask is an important part of the process of the actor's preparation for work in the character mask, which is the bridge from mask to text: the textual impulses inscribe themselves upon the *tabula rasa* the actor has prepared with the neutral mask. Copeau's move from the neutral mask to the character mask had a certain Gallic logic to it. The French tradition is that of Molière who took his training and his process from the Italian comedians, the inheritors of the masked *Commedia* tradition.

The use of character mask is based upon the idea of typicality, but it expands rather than limits. The process is technically similar to working in neutral mask. Masks are laid out in front of mirrors. The actor adopts the mask at the mirror. In rehearsal all actors go through this process, which is repeated so that all actors may try several masks. Sooner or later some response from a mask will feel right to an actor in the context of his or her own sense of the character. The actor can now explore the mask further, finding the way in which the character holds its head, gestures or walks. The walk may lead to a complete set of body rhythms; the gesture to the way in which the character focuses its energy. At this stage, the actor can explore a range of props and costume pieces appropriate to the time of the play, to find how the character might choose to handle any of these, and what response the actor gains from them.

The process of mask work is based upon the principle that we learn by osmosis. As we go through life, we develop a human vocabulary of responses, rhythms and symbologies that is stored inside us. It goes back to our atavistic roots for its impulses and has been choreographed by our instinctive response to the dynamics of living. Put simplistically, we all learn to walk downstairs; we learn by repetition and we do this with certain rhythm and energies. We adapt slightly to each stair we come across, but it is an automatic adaptation, instinctively choreographed for each occasion. We don't have to think about it, we respond; if we *did* think, we would probably trip and fall. In this way, we all make thousands of unconscious decisions every day, based upon general experience of human beings and their dynamics.

The mask reflects, literally and metaphorically, stored aspects of the human condition sculpted to produce responses in the actor. The mask does not deal in prefigured or predetermined attitudes, it produces response from the deepest wellsprings of the actor's being. The responses are manifested in activity and are very concrete. Herbert Blau has said that 'The mask's topology serves a metaphysic of psychological essences; it does not hide – it proclaims.'[4] The mask does not conceal but reveals, it does not impose, but inspires the creative imagination. Mask work in this context is part of a rehearsal process. When the actor has discovered what is useful as a character base, the mask may be discarded as more detailed work on the action proceeds. The mask, as catalyst to process, becomes the reflection of the part the actor has to play, and by an intuitive process, he or she identifies with something in the nature of the mask. The same mask will produce different characters when worn by different actors, though it will never completely change: it both confronts and responds to the actor's own personality. The process parallels stages in the conventional building of a character over a rehearsal period, ending with the assumption of costume and makeup in the dress rehearsal. The mask introduces these dynamics much sooner.

One of the great advantages of the mask process is that it is highly concrete; it can produce an active, tensile physical outline for a character. Active in a way that inner process tends not to be. The mask can make the actor freer, braver and more willing to take risks. It overthrows the limiting concept of the actor's self: the actor masks to unmask. An actor is full of masks, the character mask encourages these different aspects of personality and makes them available for the actor's use. Getting away from the singular encrusted social mask enables a deeper and fuller sense of human truths to be revealed.

The mask also encourages a heightened energy which produces

a level of potential excitement in the character. The American
critic, Dan Sullivan, has said:

> [The mask] is why we see the good actor so clearly. It's what
> we miss in the dim kind of acting that haunts the Soaps, where
> the intention seems to be to duplicate the fumbling, pause-
> strewn, sludgy buildup of ordinary life. Put these actors in
> masks, and the energy level might improve considerably.[5]

There are critics of the use of mask in the acting process. It is
said that it locks the actor into a one-dimensionality of type,
lacking psychological complexity and development. The use of
mask is only a starting point in process, and all masks have
different shadings – literally in the lights. No two actors will have
the same response; there is always the interplay between actor and
mask; and although absorption takes place, it is never absolute;
as with all great acting, there tends to be a glimpse of the actor's
self in the mask and this creates tension and energy. Development
of character from the mask is a function of the more subtle shadings and finer distinctions the actor discovers as he or she responds
to the way in which the playwright uses the character to move
the action forward.

Mask as part of the actor's process is in significant use today,
especially as a training tool, but also as a rehearsal technique.
It is interesting how the tradition has come down through the
contemporary theatre from Jacques Copeau. Michel St-Denis,
Copeau's nephew, brought it to England, through the Old Vic
School, and then it was taken to the Royal Court Theatre in the
period of Gaskill, Dexter and Keith Johnstone by George Devine.
St-Denis also took the process to his schools in Strasburg and
Montreal, and it forms a significant part of the process at the
theatre arm of the Juilliard School in New York, where St-Denis
was an advisor. In France, the tradition has been continued by
Barrault, Le Coq, Decroux and Delcroze.

It is no accident that the recovery of mask as a fundamental
theatrical artefact should have gone hand in hand with the movement away from realism – with its psychologically naturalistic
style, based upon the technique of inner process – towards a more
presentational form of theatre with a broader stylistic range. The
connection is, in fact, very specific in the person of Michel St-
Denis (whose relationship with Copeau and revival of the mask

was mentioned above) who wrote a seminal book in 1960 called *Theatre, The Rediscovery of Style*.[6] St-Denis's premise was that the actor has to come to understand, and be able to speak and act, with the particular voice of a text, and not to reduce all texts to the limitations of the actor's own voice, or the street vernacular of naturalism. The implications of this are that an actor must not simply use his or her own persona(lity), but must discover and adopt the persona of the character in the text: a character that is not a real person but a textual strategy, a *dramatis persona*, a mask of the dramatic action. Physical mask and textual mask come together in St-Denis's work. The concept has been neatly put by Richard Schechner: 'A role conforms to the logic of theatre, not the logic of any other life system. To think of a role as a person is like picnicking on a landscape painting.'[7]

The idea of the character as a fictive construct necessary to the plot structure frees the actor from the limiting idea that theatre *is* reality, rather than a reflection on, or an illusion of, reality. It is, in fact, a return to sign: the mask as a physical sign used to communicate the dynamics of action. For the actor's process, the idea of character-building as the creation of a mask of expressions, gestures, sounds and actions – everything in fact the character is physically required to do to discharge its necessary function in the play – puts the focus upon the actor's physical instrument. It does, in fact, return the idea of process back to Stanislavski, in his final perception that acting is not the engendering of feeling but the playing of physical actions.

The actor's mask of character, as a physical configuration, is created through application of the various processes we have discussed above. The shape of a particular mask will be determined by the given circumstances of a particular text: rhythm and images of speech; the character's structural function in the play (in a farce, for example, the character may be required to fall about and bump into the furniture); the manner of the physical reality of the time and place. The physical process of the building of the mask encourages playing from the actor. Overly structured internal techniques tend to ignore the vital aspect of play. That part of the birthright and communion of actors before realism's fourth wall locked them off from the audience and into themselves.

The idea that realism is more 'real' than other theatrical styles is itself a fallacy. Emotion memory as a naturalistic technique seemed to be a tool to unlock actors because, in a contemporary context, it has less distance to go in its journey of recall. It will plug into an immediate image of the life around the actor and audience: it is not obfuscated by a sense of time. Time is the pattern and coloration of style. Because Stanley Kowalski was a contemporary of Marlon Brando, or Marlon Brando was a contemporary of Stanley Kowalski, Brando could the more easily adapt Kowalski's mask to his own persona – the actor's problem of adapting to other times, manners, places is less acute. Brando's mask may have appeared more 'real'; it was just more contemporary. And it was no less a mask than that, say, of Horner, the great Restoration 'stud'. We don't immediately see Horners around us, because his clothes, manner of speech, sensibility and environment are all seventeenth century. But we recognize a Horner. The actor has an intuitive sense of the dynamics of the character, his further task is then to situate him appropriately in the circumstances of the text. Horner is less contemporary but *qua* character dynamics and *qua qua* aesthetically is no less 'real' than Kowalski who, in any case, will become as distant, but no less 'real,' as a Horner in three hundred years' time.

John Mortimer has well expressed the differences between an aesthetic approach to an art form and a purely realistic perspective: 'To catch some fleeting truths in a web of artifice rather than banging them over the head with a camera and tape recorder.'[8] In the actor's process, that 'web of artifice' becomes wholly concrete when the character is thought of as the physical creation of a mask. And, as the character is created from the textual impulses and given circumstances of the play, and not from the personal parameters of the actor, the problems of adaptation to style become much easier for the actor to deal with. The topology of the mask will reflect the different demands and dynamics of different plays.

Chapter 8

The dynamics of acting: style

As John Gielgud has said, style is knowing what kind of a play you are in. The idea of style tended to have a bad press during the naturalistic period, especially in the United States, to the degree that a respected member of the profession, Uta Hagen, could call it the dirtiest word in the business. Style became associated with artificiality, and thus dishonesty, because of the actor's failure to understand and respect the demands and dynamics of given circumstances which revealed the nature of a text. The received perception that an actor had to be him- or herself (as opposed to creating a mask of character by selection and adaptation), led to the idea of style as artificial embroidery rather than the warp and woof of the text. Actors spent time upon emotion memory to make themselves sweat on stage if the 'day' were hot, but failed to take into account the structure and rhythms of the language, theatrical and social conventions, and the tone of the play as inculcated by the social, political and moral energies of the playwright, all of which are intrinsic to the play's structure. Text not only provides the actor with the impulses to action but the shape of that action: the signs and signals that communicate a particular style in accordance with the given circumstances of the text.

The recovery of mask, both as *dramatis persona* and physical process, was both demanded by and made possible the broad spectrum of stylistic endeavours, such as absurdism, and the work of Brecht and Artaud, which distinguished the post-realist period of the 1950s and 1960s. The determination of style, the final vital and concrete nature of the *mise-en-scène* has, in our century, become the prerogative of the director. But the actor must realize this by specific choices of action, moment by moment. 'Knowing what kind of a play you are in' – how the world of the play affects choices and, not infrequently, demands certain responses if the dynamics and rhythms of the text are to be validly realized – is a crucial part of the acting process: the creation of the right mask for a particular event.

That texts *do* have the dynamics of a particular world printed within them was brought home to me quite recently when in rehearsal for the production of a Coward play. The universal use of the cigarette as a sophisticated social prop in the 1920s and 1930s informs the atmosphere of Coward's work. Indeed, it is part of the punctuation of the language, predicated upon the inhaling and exhaling of smoke, and the flicking of ash – just as the language of the seventeenth- and eighteenth-century comedies was written for the fan. Coward's play was being rehearsed in one of the socially-conscious, smoke-free theatres of the western United States, and cigarettes on stage were *verboten*. A young actor, intuiting in the rhythms of the text the need for a prop, brought an apple on stage and made a brave attempt to eat it in response to the rhythmical punctuation of the text. Alas! The choice was intrinsically foreign to the play. Quite apart from the fact that the very 'sign' of an apple is fresh, earthy, innocent and un-Coward-like, it cannot be handled like a cigarette. It takes too long to bite, too long to chew, gets in the way of sharp, staccato consonants, is quite unflickable, and the core presents a problem.

This may seem like a trivial example, and I am sure that when Coward has been thoroughly deconstructed (or defumigated) his stage may become littered with apple cores – not to mention assorted ethnic virgins with flowers in their hair – but it does speak to the actor's crucial task of making appropriate choices within the demands of the text.

Harold Pinter, actor before playwright, both created a stylistic problem for the contemporary actor and provided the solution. As actor David Baron, Pinter toured with one of the last actor-managers and was introduced to the tradition of the making of 'dramatic moments' by the actor: the sweep of a cloak, the swirl of a sword, the pose at the door – what would now be regarded as the fustian signs of a dated style or, in a word, 'ham'. Pinter recognized, however, that such moments were theatrically important in lifting theatre above the flat, undifferentiated plane of everyday existence: they were a part of 'acting' as opposed to simply 'being'. In his plays, Pinter found a way of accommodating the dramatic gesture to a small domestic world by using time and space to frame the ordinary, everyday gesture. Thus, the handling of a newspaper, the drinking of a glass of water, the crossing of legs within the structure of Pinter's language and silence, create the equivalent effect of the cloak and dagger menace of a less diminished day.

Pinter presents another interesting problem to the actor brought up on the Stanislavski concept of a rational through-line of character: the principle of nonverifiability, especially of the past. An actor's process cannot be rigid; it must be sufficiently broad and eclectic to adapt to the demands of any particular playwright. It is here that the concept of a mask constructed as a sign which represents and reflects the features of a text at any moment in time, is more useful than the idea of a psyche, which might drive the inner engine of the actor but not necessarily along the road map of the play.

The principle of nonverifiability – the impossibility of ever being certain of what happened in the past – opens up the possibility of constantly creating new pasts in the present. Pinter's characters do this. They employ the reconstruction of different versions of the past as strategies in the present. The audience can never know with certainty what is 'true', but is affected by the pattern the strategies create. All are struggling with uncertainty – actor, character, audience – within the void at the centre of our existence: the lack of fixed points in a relativistic, constantly changing world. As Yeats has described the modern condition in *The Second Coming*:

Things fall apart; the centre cannot hold;
Mere anarchy is loosed upon the world

How can a character have a core, a consistency of self in such circumstances? But the actor is not left in a state of anarchy. The actor's process can still be applied to justifying in the moment the sometimes contradictory attitudes of the character. Pinter's actors search for the mask, constructed of possible pasts, that will operate most successfully in the current moment of the play. The mask is a complex(ion) of these moment-to-moment choices which achieve the character's strategy. This is quite different from the playing of shadings of a consistent psychological self based upon a rational through-line of motivation. Through the process of revision, Pinter's characters – like actors themselves – create the role that will give them tactical supremacy.

If this adaptation of the actor's process is necessary in Pinter, it is even more so in the approach to the absurdist writers of the 1950s and 1960s, where irrationality and lack of a determined self is a basic principle (if such there is) of the playwright's work. And, indeed, the idea of a character being created by the complex of actions it played throughout its journey within the play is not new to the second half of this century. It has sometimes troubled Bradleyesque modern criticism of Shakespeare that, for example, Prince Hal rejects Falstaff, or that Cleopatra is both hussy and queen. Elizabethan actors, without benefit of Descartes, Freud or Stanislavski, would have found no difficulty with such role-playing – it being a given of Shakespeare's work. While an actor can never know how many children Lady Macbeth had, even if it were a useful enquiry, what the actor does know is that she 'has given suck', and would have 'dashed the child's brains out' before being as pusillanimous as Macbeth: two extremely vital, physical, and playable resources for her mask. Madeleine Doran has put the point well:

> That [Elizabethan actors] operated by no formal theory of individuality of character, except perhaps the humour theory, is shown by the frequent failure of coherence of character. . . . This of itself need not mean a lack of expressive energy. . . . the sense of living wholeness we recognize in the depiction of all successful individual characters may be present merely in intensely realized situations.[1]

The process of acting is no more a monolith than is theatre itself. Mask or face is, finally, an invalid dichotomy. The performer is both the actor and the character. Supremely conscious of the duality, and supremely adept at using both illusion and non-illusion, Shakespeare makes a comment on it in *A Midsummer Night's Dream* (Act III, Scene i):

> *Bottom*: Why then may you leave a casement of the great chamber, where we play, open, and the Moon may shine in at the casement.
> *Quince*: Ay, or else one must come in with a bush of thorns

and a lanthorn and say he comes to disfigure, or to
present the person of Moonshine.

The interaction of illusion and nonillusion, a fundamental precept
of theatre – and increasingly of life – is equivalent to the way in
which the faces or masks of actor and character blend or conflict.
Acting is neither 'being' nor 'feeling', though it may include both:
it is a series of appropriate practices or processes in response to
a text, or other starting point; it is different masks for different
tasks. This is what makes possible both permutations upon a role,
and the variations of style.

In our time, perhaps Bertolt Brecht is the most obvious example
of how the use of mask is crucial to the acting process. Not
only has Brecht used actual masks in his productions, but the
fundamental task for the actor in his work – finding the appropriate
gestus – is based on the evident separation or 'estrangement' of the
actor from the mask of character, so that the audience can recognize in the actor's performance a criticism of the character presented. The acceptance of the essentially public and artificial (i.e.
created by artifice) nature of theatrical performance, puts the
Brechtian actor's process at the opposite end of the spectrum from
the Stanislavskian actor, seen as trying hard to build a 'real'
human being from the structure of his or her own emotional
responses, with which the audience will empathize.

As Brecht himself has required, the actor 'narrates the story of
his character' and is free to criticize and, to enhance the dialectical
nature of Brecht's work, to contradict the character he or she
plays. The actor builds the role from a social perspective, and
does not look for emotional or psychological motivation but for
the social gist (or *gestus*) of the part. The question Brecht's actor
will ask is not 'Who am I?' but 'What [i.e. social function] am
I?' It is the consequences of the action in sociopolitical terms that
concern Brecht; not the psychical nature of the self. Again, an
actor will not ask 'Is a capitalist a capitalist because he or she is
anally retentive or sexually impotent?'; but 'What is the social and
economic effect of being a capitalist?' That *gestus* is then played in
the mask of the character in such a manner that the audience will
appreciate the critical stance of the actor.

The demands of the character mask do not prevent the actor
exploring the situation in any way he or she finds useful – Brecht

used a lot of improvisation – but final choices will be made in terms of social not psychological behaviour. The demands of the fable – the telling of the narrative of the story – will always supersede any elaboration of personal characteristics. The actor does not look for emotion, but will accept whatever is present and channel it into the objective playing of the action. It is thus externalized and becomes living energy in the presentation of the *gestus*, it is not internalized and subjectively examined.

It is only through a physical process of building a mask or creating a *gestus* (or sign) that an actor can approach Brecht's work. An even more intensely physical process of the creation of sign was demanded by one of Brecht's contemporaries, Antonin Artaud, whose concept of a 'Theatre of Cruelty' was one of the most dynamic influences upon the post-realistic theatre. 'Cruelty' implied an intensity and severity of communication calculated to drain the ulcer of humanity's suppressed desires and instincts, which Artaud believed to be held in, suppurating beneath the masks of bourgeois behaviour. Cruelty is, above all, rigour; Artaud called for intense physical images, and suggested that actors should be like martyrs, burning alive but signalling through the flames.

Artaud himself was, perhaps, more a visionary than practitioner – being medically disabled from working for many years – and he left no sense of process for the actor. It was Jerzy Grotowski, his most faithful acolyte, who developed a series of stringent exercises to support the demands of Cruelty.

Actors were the prime focus of his theatre. Grotowski called his process *via negativa*. Its intention was not so much to build a physical mask as to strip the actor of all blocks, resistances and simplistic stereotypes. In *Towards a Poor Theatre*, Grotowski urges the actor to ask: 'What are the obstacles blocking you on your way to the total act which must engage all your psychophysical resources?'[2] He suggests that the impulses received by the actor from 'confronting' the text would inculcate in the actor a score of actions, gestures and sounds, and this organic system of signs would embrace the audience, who would then share the intensity of the actor's experience.

The actor is not trying, through this process, to find the detailed and specific responses of a character in terms of any biographical detail. But neither is the actor performing simply in his or her own persona. Through responses to the impulses of the text, the actor's body becomes part of the 'signals through the flames' of which Artaud spoke: a sign or hieroglyph as part of the total sign of the *mise-en-scène* – not unlike the way (though by a different process) the Brechtian actor finds a sign or *gestus* that relates to the total *gestus* of the scene. The signs discovered by the Artaudian actor are neither psychological nor pantomimic; they have a resonance beyond any realistic gesture, finding their source in humanity's deepest, most atavistic cultural associations – the collective unconscious of which Jung spoke.

As physical signs in themselves, the actor's process is enhanced by the significant use of properties. Not the bric-à-brac of realism such as cigarettes, glasses, cups and saucers (the actor in the Artaudian process does not 'measure out his life in coffee spoons') but properties with a less specific identity cloth, rope, nets, staves – which, by the way they are used by the actor, may take on a highly symbolic signature, as the wafer and wine of the Christian Mass become the flesh and blood of Christ. Through gesture an actor can turn blue silk into a lake; a stool into an altar; a piece of glass into a teardrop. One of the more memorable gestures by an actor in this style was in Peter Brook's production of the *Marat/Sade* when Glenda Jackson, as Charlotte Corday, flagellated de Sade with her hair.

Grotowski's process of manifesting Artaud's style recalls the biomechanical theories of Meyerhold, and is a further illustration of the principle of body memory associated with William James and Moshe Feldenkrais: that memories are always a physical reaction. Every emotion, in one way or another, is linked in the cerebral cortex with some muscular configuration and attitude that has the power of reinstating the responses to a prior situation. It is the principle upon which rehearsal is based: the incarnation in body memory of the choices the actor makes. Through the actor's process, the text becomes a score of physical actions inspired by and attached to impulses. While the score is fixed, it is not without spontaneity because the body, in revealing its encoded signs, is at the same time responding to the stimulus of the moment. Once more there is the margin of play whereby the signs are played by the actor in the context not only of the learned score, but in that of each specific performance and its given circumstances. As in life: each time we repeat something it is the same, but slightly different.

The Artaudian process is probably the most ideographic, ideated and idealistic attempt at the total use of the actor as physical sign. In Artaud's metaphysicality neither actor nor role changes each other. It is the mutual discoveries of their confrontations – the *sign* of mythic *sign*ificance, the *sign*al through the flames sparked by the intense encounter, fusion or conflagration of actor and text – that embraces, consumes, purifies and liberates the audience.

From the above discussion of the dynamics of acting one could deduce that acting is skills applied through process to create style. This might be useful at the level of rhetoric, and is the kind of exegesis that one always feels compelled to come out with in a book of this nature. However, it is perhaps closer to praxis to say that acting, finally, is what works: it is process not system. This would allow for the necessary eclecticism and flexibility that the idea of process presumes. The nature of process will often depend upon the demands of a particular role. While 'good acting' will always entail authenticity of communication, this will not necessarily be of the actor's self. But it will demand authentic communication of the text, and this can mean not one but several authentic masks of the actor to encompass different levels of textual circumstance.

The *Marat/Sade* provides an example of various levels of demand upon the actor within one performance. At one level the actor is playing a mad person, someone incarcerated in an insane asylum for a personality disturbance. The actor will presumably employ some kind of naturalistic process to discover and play elements associated clinically with the mad person's problem. Beyond this, in a Brechtian mode, the actor/mad person is playing a character in the French Revolution, and passing an ironical and critical comment upon the character's political function. Further beyond this, the actor/mad person/political character is asked to perform an Artaudian function as part of an ensemble which jointly creates signs or hieroglyphs of faces and forces of the revolution itself: violence, terror, greed, sexuality – 'No revolution without general copulation'. Thus, to communicate the authenticity of a text, an actor may have to perform not one authentic self, but several authentic (to the action) masks.

To return for a moment to the idea of realism with its received presumption of naturalistic process. The attempt at a recapitulation of the individual's psychological and emotional response to the everyday exigencies of a contemporary environment (or 'to hold a mirror up to nature') will always be with us. We have, as human beings, somehow learned to be enormously self-conscious; possibly because we are no longer sure of what that self is, now that it seems not to be an immediate reflection of God's image. Curiosity about ourselves as individuals – how we work psychologically in a private way (something that can fit on to a television screen), and whether we can learn anything from the way in which people who look just like us work – will continue to be with us; especially now that technology can pretend to look into our soul through the eye of a camera, and reflect it upon a screen. So, the naturalistic process is, like death and taxes, here to stay, though its vocabulary of signs will change. Realism already presents us with a taxonomic problem. It is both a reflection of reality – what we think we see everyday – and the name applied to a style at the end of the nineteenth century which, in many respects, no longer looks anything like what we do see every day! Ironically, realism is slippery; it is always moving on us, and even the most determined attempt to present its face will soon find a mask on its hands.

The term 'authentic', rather than variations of 'real' with its imputations of observable 'truths', may be more useful in talking of the acting experience. It is quite possible that, in certain forms of naturalistic acting – especially in first performances of new plays – the audience can be given an authentic experience of the actor's self: the self precisely fits the demands of the text; it is the mask of character. This experience must merit the term 'good acting'. Though even here there are problems for the idea that the actor's authentic face can ever be the communicative sign. The concept of mimesis, as applied to character, presumes a given self that imitates something else. Today the very idea of a concrete self is problematical; it may be more a question of which of the actor's masks of self fits what mask of character at any given moment of action. Equally, the idea that the actor can present his or her authentic self to the audience ignores the inevitable mediation of theatrical environment. Louise Page, a writer associated with the naturalistic process of acting has said,

I don't think you ever go out and meet any of the characters

I've written on the street, because there is a point where they are not quite characters, they are also metaphors or images.[3]

Or masks, we might add, whose contours reflect essences of existence. Actors draw from the range of possible persons they have within them, to reveal truths about our world that are both beneath and beyond 'real' physiognomical detail. They select from the palette of selves available to us all; rather than attempting to define and hold in place the functional daily mask we like to think of as our self.

Much of contemporary theatre has, of course, been concerned with the *auth*or's negation of the idea of an *auth*entic self, reinforcing what we perceive as the phenomenological dichotomy of the actor. This problem seems to be resolved by the concept of mask: both the spectrum of possible masks, and the range of degrees of fusion of the actor with the mask. Ironically, the more the human being is perceived of as a role player and mask-wearer, the more the process of the discovery and wearing of masks will create an authenticity for the act of acting: it will equate with the life process – mask on mask.

This concept goes hand in hand with the idea of text as process. Regarded not so much as a high wire from which the actor may fall, but a trampoline. Both firm base and safety net, yet a flexible membrane (memory brain?) from which the actor can spring to feats of derring-dramatic-do, and return to find ever-renewed impulses. Just as the trampoline is not rigid, neither will be the mask. The actor may choose that leap at any moment which best serves the potential of the textual trampoline. Thus playing the action which finds its source in the text reveals the skill of the actor in creating the appropriate sign, and draws on his or her total resources. In playing the action fully – fulfilling the dynamics of the leap – the mask will reveal and catalyse, not conceal and restrict. Thus for skill and process; but style is also served by the metaphor. The size, shape and tensile nature of the trampoline (the given circumstances of the text) will influence the manner and shape of the actor's leap – the dynamics of his or her performance – and contribute to the style of the event.

What, if anything, can or should be said by way of summation of this discourse on dynamics of acting; this prattle about praxis? Acting is what the actor does. Every scene in every play has, within the text, an implicit physical shape which will be realized by the way actors move and relate in a determined space. The shape is the outcome of the impulses to action, contained in the emotional, psychological and structural dynamics of the language, as they work within the parameters of the space. Where actors go is a product of what they want to achieve, within the articulation of the *mise-en-scène*.

By testing the text – tapping into the deep structure where the impulses lie – the actor translates impulses into an action/sign, heightened by imagination and personal chemistries, and clarified and focused by technique. The impulses are received by the audience as a mask of character – re-expressed textual impulses – operating within the shape of the total *mise-en-scène*: the physical re-expression of the total shape of the textual action. It is the creation of a conscious mask from subconscious impulses.

Actors expose themselves to their roles, confronting and plumbing both the text and their own human potential, and expressing the essence through a technical structure. Without the technical structure of the mask, the communication will be blurred – feeling without form does not create a communicable sign. Equally, while feeling is useless without form, form must not get in the way of feeling. The form itself must be clear, economical and direct or it will diffuse the impact of feeling.

The brilliance, the power of the sign, will be determined by the capacity of the actor's instrument to communicate: the force of the actor's personal Gestalt. What is it about the actor that will influence the effectiveness of the sign he or she creates? First, there will be the body itself, its shape and what I have called athletic skills. Then comes the shape of the actor's psyche and range of the emotional palette. No less important is the actor's curiosity, ability to open and absorb experience, willingness to take risks, to go where the impulse leads, to expose and reveal the way in which experience works within the actor.[4] Then there are the actor's imagination, energy and sexual chemistry. More mundanely, but no less important for a working actor, is the ability to work within structure, be it of the text or the production company, and not to be restricted by it. Finally, there is the strength of the actor's need to test and experience the shared identity of humankind and its sense of eternity; to personify in all their dimensionality the spirit or 'spirits' of their time, and never to be satisfied; to attempt always to sense the insensible, touch the intangible, to 'f' the ineffable.

Whatever ultimate necessity may lie in the metaphysical dimension of acting, to return to earth it must be said that the act of acting is seen in action. Some of the language used above – 'expose', 'confront', 'respond', 'reveal' and 'risk' – suggests this practicality. Further, the language of rehearsal betrays the ever-present demands of doing: give, take, cheat, push, pull, attack, simmer, bring to a boil. Perhaps there is no better reminder of both the metaphor and mundanity of acting than in the words of two great practitioners: Edith Evans 'It's all a great big glass tube and you blow down it'; and Ralph Richardson 'It's the knack of keeping a large roomful of people from coughing.'

Chapter 9

The cybernetics of acting: space and design

As was suggested in the discussion of semiotics, in a very important sense what makes acting 'acting', in the theatrical intention of the term, is the framework of the occasion which surrounds it: concretely, the performance space.

The section on process concluded that the actor finds the impulses in a text which impel him or her to a realization of the emotional shape of the action in terms of the physical shape of the space. Inevitably, this process will be affected by the articulation of the ground plan and the total physical shape and size of the stage and auditorium: the relationship this sets up between actor and actor, and actor and audience.

I had an illustration of that some years ago when some young actors, who had been used to working in a 200-seat house with a 35-foot proscenium opening, were translated into a 600-seat house with a 70-foot proscenium for a production of *The Importance of Being Earnest*. Jack and Algy had, at first, the greatest difficulty in accepting that they could still carry on a close relationship while sitting 15 feet apart. They had to be sent to the back of the house to look at stage managers sitting in their places, before they could accept that the sign of closeness received by the audience was relative to the total space, and that intimacy is a function of an emotional not spatial relationship. In somewhat opposite terms, this was one of the fallacies of the environmental staging of the 1960s and 1970s, whereby all space belonged to both actors and audience; or the actors violated audience space in the service of closer communion. It was quickly discovered that to put one's arms around a person is not necessarily to embrace him or her in any emotional sense; and to surround the audience with the performance does not necessarily mean touching it in any greater depth than in a proscenium theatre.

There has, in this century, been a significant concern with the achievement of an optimal theatrical space – a function of the fact that we are both the benefactors of two thousand years of theatrical history, and are burdened with its architectural baggage. Greek theatrical space was an organic representation of the need of Greek dramatic form. Elizabethan dramatic form and space were intrinsically related, and the same may be said of the court theatres of the seventeenth and early eighteenth centuries. Then, in the bourgeois and popular periods, economic and social dynamics rather than the inherent physical demands of a play tended to shape theatrical spaces, which led to a homogenization of physical style.

The historical sensibility of the late nineteenth century began to reconsider the relationship of text to space. Granville Barker, for example, showed that Shakespeare wrote for a particular theatrical space, and his plays may only be completely realizable in such a space. This reconstruction of the nature of theatrical space led to the experimentation, particularly in the latter half of this century, and to the thrust stages which Tyrone Guthrie was instrumental in developing, and arena stages after the energies of Stephen Joseph.

Today, the actor can expect to be faced with performing in a wide gamut of spaces; anything from a 2,000-seat proscenium house to a film studio with a camera and a group of technicians 3 feet away from their face. How will the contemporary actor's work be affected by different spaces as he or she pursues a career amid the architectural bric-à-brac into which the inherited repertory of the late twentieth century once organically fitted? Certainly an adjustment will have to be made between performances, not only in the extreme situations quoted above, but in a proscenium, a thrust, or an arena space. But will the adjustment be one of technique; or does something change in the nature of acting?

While the twentieth century has been attempting to find the optimal space into which the vast differentiated repertory of its inheritance might fit, there is as much chance of that as there is that an optimal acting style could be evolved that would equally serve that repertory. As mentioned previously, John Gielgud has said that style is 'knowing what kind of a play you are in'. In the first instance, of course, the problem of style is one for the director and designer. But in the final instance, it is the actor who bears the burden of communicating a play to an audience within the parameters of a given space which may now be quite unlike that for which the play was conceived. This does present a problem for the actor. To take an extreme example: how does the actor handle an aside in an arena space? To take it four times, once to each segment of the audience, would rather shatter the convention that the other characters are unaware.

Again, the nature of the audience–actor relationship intended by the Shakespearean soliloquy will be significantly altered in a large proscenium house, though Shakespeare has been successfully mounted in such spaces. So it is not being said that a play can only be performed in the space the playwright had in mind; although it is probably best performed in such a space. Greek drama illustrates this point. Infrequently performed today, because of this very problem of its inherent stylistic demands, it has been produced without masks and in spaces other than the original relationship of actor and chorus to audience. If masks are not used and a more intimate space involved, the absolutely determined formality of the drama will be tempered and acting must reflect this. But the fundamental dynamics of the play will not have changed. It won't suddenly have become 'realistic' dealing with the minutiae of daily life and psychological detail of character. Greek drama was written for the iconic dynamics of the mask; characters were essentially archetypes not emanations of well-rounded psyches. The concerns of Greek tragedy were with large ethical issues, with gods and Fate. The issues determine the structure and the structure supports the style. The actor must be aware of this in order to come to terms with what the dynamics of the play are asking him or her to do within the dynamics of a given space. 'Knowing what kind of a play you are in' is crucial if the actor is to accommodate and not travesty.

Without belabouring the issue, the same exercise will apply for the actor whenever the voice of the play is to be communicated in a space for which it was not written. Again, it is not being said that plays cannot receive perfectly good productions with spatial and stylistic reinterpretation. Indeed, with the currency of deconstruction at a premium upon the critical exchange, one would be hard put to suggest rendering purely unto Caesar the things that are Caesar's. But, if one might borrow from the Las Vegas syndrome of architectural post-modernism, the actor should try to avoid rendering the things that are Caesar's into the image of Caesar's Palace.

The actor's relationship to space reinforces the proposition that acting is a process. The actor's mask, as sculpted by the impulses of the text, will be further articulated to the dynamics of the space – a cybernetic process. At its simplest level, it is the way in which an actor on tour tries out the size and resonance of the house before the curtain goes up, so that the actor's vocal dynamics may be adjusted to its feel. And, with the voice, so goes the Gestalt of the physical mask. The ability to reconcile the shape of text and space is part of the necessary process and instinct of the professional.

There will always be some trade-off in this process – something lost and something gained: less structure of convention, more freedom to play; more intimacy, less total control. It is all part of the 'stock' exchange of the actor's business; and it isn't always easy. The actor can feel he or she has two left feet or not enough heads while the adjustment is being made, as it must be, to the size and shape of whatever frame is defining the dynamics of the actor's performance at any given time.

Perhaps the greatest trade-off for the stage actor comes with exposure to the most intimate frame of all, that of the camera. All kinds of contradictions have to be reconciled. The vastness of the studio space has nothing to do with what the camera records. The actor quickly discovers that a physical movement of a foot on stage requires only an inch on camera – hence the adage that stage actors are too big for the camera – until they adjust. Yet this miniaturization of technique ends up as enormous exaggeration of detail when blown up on the screen, where the audience is metaphorically breathing down the actor's neck – as were the technicians in the studio.

It is perhaps an amusing irony that film, regarded as the most realistic medium of all, is in many ways inimical to the basic concepts of a naturalistic process. Certainly there is a cheek-by-jowl intimacy in the final results seen by the audience; and the camera in close-up records the innermost details of the actor's thoughts and inner process. The triumph of Stanislavski, one might think. In fact, the broken nature of the shooting process: short scenes out of narrative order, and endlessly reshot; close-ups which have to be cheated for the camera with little or no spatial relationship to the master shot. All of this makes for the impossibility of building any through-line of action or character, and lends itself better to the putting on and off of a mask of character at a moment's notice, and adapting that mask to the technological demands of the space, namely the studio and its technology. A process that is in keeping with our earlier inferences.

So far this discussion has been concerned with how acting is affected by the structural parameters of space. Equally important to the actor's work is the interior design of that space. Perhaps the most dynamic factor influencing this in modern theatre is the use of lighting. Before the advent of electric lighting, the illumination of the acting space was relatively simple; either daylight outdoors or some form of candle or oil lighting inside the theatre. Before the nineteenth century this tended to mean that the actor sought the downstage, particularly downstage centre – areas where candle, oil pot or chandelier would be. This affected the shape of acting, giving it a somewhat flat, horizontal and rhetorical quality. Not only did the use of electric lighting enable interior space of a theatre to be articulated in ways that made the architectural form less dominant, but, through the initial influence of directors such as Adolph Appia and Gordon Craig, it gave the actor a three-dimensional fluidity in space. This has put greater emphasis upon the actor's body, particularly as it relates to the depth of space, and other artefacts in the *mise-en-scène*. The actor now has nowhere to hide, unless the stage action calls for it: the actor may be brightly lit in any part of the space. This has created for the actor a much stronger sense of ensemble, a relationship at all times to other actors – not a question of simply finding the downstage light, giving the line and then relinquishing focus to the next speaker. Acting now requires an instinctive sense of the total stage picture, and an ability to counter to retain this balance without destroying focus. Electric light has brought a tremendous reinforcement to the actor, in terms of creating focus and enhancing the mood and psychological dimensions of the moment. It asks in return for a sophisticated, but understated awareness from the actor of where his or her light is; when to take it; and how, at all times, he or she relates to the total stage action and shape of the *mise-en-scène*.

If lighting can now determine the shape of interior acting space, the shape of action within it will be determined by the design of the space – the nature and placement of the stage furniture and properties. This, together with the way in which the actor is dressed, will have a crucial effect upon the way in which the actor creates and displays the character mask. We have already suggested that an actor finds impulses towards action from his or her response to the text. The way in which those impulses are expressed in movement will be determined by the shape of the ground plan – the way in which the interior space of the stage is determined by the placement of set pieces, properties and furniture. In very simplistic terms, the way in which an actor moves from point A to point B will be determined by what is in his or her path. If there is a sofa, the actor cannot move directly – unless the sofa is leapt over, which may well be allowable if the character is eccentric or if the play is a farce. This goes right to the heart of the matter of design as it reinforces or determines the style of a production and, therefore, the opportunities and limitations given the actor.

We have mentioned the importance to the actor of knowing what kind of a play you are in, which, in the context of design, means knowing how to work optimally upon anything from a bare stage, though abstract, symbolic or fragmentary settings to the fully built, three-dimensional, fourth wall demands of realism. Today, an actor may be confronted by Shakespeare's Forest of Arden that has to be drawn in the audience's imagination, on a bare stage, by the use of language alone; or that may be a gobo of leaves, hanging ropes, metal sculptures, fabric drapes, or even painted trees. The actor has to know how to relate to any of these, and what dynamics of voice and gesture are called for. The more the setting is unlocalized or advertises theatricality, the less naturalistic will be the performance required of the actor. It can be as simple as the fact that an actor cannot open a door that isn't there, but must still define an exit. Or, the more one is dealing with painted flats, the less a door that *is* there may be banged shut.

Fully dressed, realistic environments in some respects seem to ask the least of the actor, as they provide all the necessary givens of the action and bring their own vocabulary of usage with them. The task seems to be fulfilling the audience's expectation of how such everyday artefacts are used. In fact, for the imaginative actor, a realistic setting offers great opportunity for discovering interesting and varied choices without destroying the illusion of reality.

For example, there is many more than one way of sitting in a chair: upright, slouched, astride, sidesaddle, reversed with the arms on the back. The same principle applies to relating to someone on a sofa, or around a table. And to the use of properties – a telephone, a coffeepot, a cup and saucer may all be used with variety and inventiveness, adding dimensionality to character and interest to everyday moments of action. What is being said is that, finally, for the actor the set is a playground, filled with playthings that challenge the imagination and allow for improvisational use. The investment of the ordinary with interest, without transgressing the parameters of style, is a touchstone of good acting.

Opportunities afforded to the actor by the set design are enhanced by the costume design – the way in which the actor's body is clothed: which becomes, of course, a direct part of the actor's character mask. Costume will be related to the style of the production and will require and encourage the actor to move as the nature of the environment or period dictates. The most obvious effect upon the actor will be made by clothes from periods quite different from his or her own: the Elizabethan and seventeenth and eighteenth centuries for example. Here the actor will have heavy clothing, wide-skirted jackets and dresses, wigs, fans, swords and snuffboxes to deal with. All of which, again, can either be regarded as an encumbrance or relished by the actor for the acting opportunities they afford. The actor may not now be allowed to improvise so freely in sitting on a chair – the clothing and conventions of the time forbidding this – but other elements of costume can be used creatively. The fan, for example, is the most marvellous conversational weapon for the actress. For the actor, quite apart from the way in which he displays his leg, the way in which he uses the skirts of his jacket can say much about a character; and the snuffbox affords almost as much opportunity to the man as the fan does to the woman. The sniff critical, the sniff military, the sniff foppish, the sniff flirtatious, etc., will all be part of the vocabulary of the creative actor.

In sum, the space within which an actor works, and how that space is articulated, lighted and designed, has an enormous impact upon the actor's work. For the able actor, a move is never merely a way of getting from A to B; a prop is never just utilitarian: both are opportunities for improvisation, creativity and revelation of character. Playing: the creation of interesting choices within the emotional and stylistic parameters of the action – variety without contrivance, economy without loss of interest, comfort without lack of style – are all marks of acting which will be put into high relief by an actor's response to the dynamics of design with which he or she is working.

Chapter 10

The cybernetics of acting: director and rehearsal

The first contact an actor will have with the space is where the process takes place – in the rehearsal room. In fact, when an actor is working on a part, the rehearsal process will take place wherever he or she may be – in bed, in the bath, on the bus, in the bar – but, formally, it will be in the rehearsal room. Just as an actor's process is personal, so will be the way in which rehearsal is approached. The process will be affected by the nature of the play; the relationships established with fellow actors and the director; and the time available for the work. But, underlying all of this there are some factors common to the nature of rehearsal that affect the acting experience.

The most fundamental factor is probably the 'sharing' of rehearsal. Unlike most other art forms, acting cannot be done alone, and 'working' in the society of fellow actors is what an actor is about. So much time is spent in solitariness – waiting for work, looking for work, competing for work – that the blessed experience of sharing the creative endeavour, even when the play is rubbish, affirms the actor's sense of worth and purpose. At early rehearsals, when fellow actors are yet unknown quantities and somewhat self-protective at exposing their abilities, or lack of, to each other, there is still the shared familiarity of the dingy rehearsal room with its predictable jetsam of props, and tea or coffee provided by the ever-nurturing stage management. This produces a sense of expectation and fulfilment; all know why the others are there and what each has had to fight through in order to be there.

Such an atmosphere lends an immediately positive quality to the necessary sharing of rehearsal. The awareness of fellow actors probably takes a threefold form. First, as a member of the community of actors, there for the purpose of creating something which all are ultimately to launch upon an audience: the need for mutual support in face of this future hazard. Second, as specific actors: people who will be discovered to have certain qualities and who work in a particular way. Then, gradually, as a character in the play who responds to your character. Two fractured uncertainties have to offer, take, feel each other out, while building masks that agree to be mutually responsive to each other and form part of the larger fabric of the play. Knowing the other actor as a person keeps a strong sense of reality in the rehearsal situation while watching the process of the evolution of the character reinforces the sense of wonder and play.

The acting profession is often regarded as superficial or artificial in the elaborateness of its mutual endearments and the ease of its physical contact. But, inevitably, close relationships must develop between actors over the period of rehearsal. In the first place, there has to be an immediate willingness to give in order that the emotional intimacy of the play may be encompassed in a relatively short time. Then there is that trust and presumption of mutual protection, based upon the unspoken but subconscious knowledge that they are not normal people, but actors who bear (depending upon the point of view) the mark of Cain or the kiss of Calliope. The necessary closeness of the rite of passage (which is what a rehearsal fundamentally is) derives from an experience that is unique to actors: part need, part support, part joy, part fear – and total sharing of the mystery.

The degree of closeness and sharing achieved by the actors in rehearsal will depend significantly upon the working atmosphere created by the director. But the nature of the actor–director relationship will inevitably differ from that between the actors themselves. This is a function of the fact that their ultimate purposes are different, and whatever the risks taken by the director in rehearsal, it is finally the actors alone who have to face the audience, while the director sits, however nervously, at the back of the orchestra, or paces about the bar.

The director has become such an important figure in this production process, and legends of directorial prowess so abound in our time (from Saxe-Meiningen's 'invention' of crowd scenes, through Craig's 'invention' of symbolic scenic plasticity, Reinhardt's *Regiebücher* and Peter Brook's improvisational inventiveness) that one tends to forget that only 'in our time' has the director taken a major place in the theatre. Indeed, it was only in 1937 that the Comédie Française began to name directors in its programmes; while the term 'producer', by implication a much less direct function, was used by the British theatre until quite recently. There are, indeed, many actors who still believe the director to be an unnecessary intrusion upon work best left to them: 'Why don't they let actors act?' is a plaintive cry.

James Agate, the early twentieth-century critic, was of the opinion that the only two arts of theatre were playwrighting and acting, and no third art was needed to co-ordinate them. Why then is a director necessary, and what is his or her effect upon the acting process? Basically, and simplistically, a director has two functions: interpretation and integration. Integration is a function of the enormous growth of technology and consequently of range of possibility and choices in the theatre. Every element of production, from space through lighting, costuming, set and sound design, is no longer a given but a choice. Thus, at the very simplest level, if a degree of consistency of style and effect is to be achieved, someone has to be able to integrate the choices in accordance with some sense of how the play is to be presented and perceived. The 'sense' is the interpretational side of the director's function. He or she will be guided in the integration of choices by a 'concept', an idea of how the audience is to experience the play.

Here again, interpretation as a conscious function is something of a modern idea, born of the fact that we now have a large inherited repertory of plays which may be permutated with the available range of technology and design. Whereas Shakespeare was on hand to explain, if necessary, his plays to the known company of actors, who performed on a given stage, in given costumes to a relatively known audience, today there is an enormous range of possibilities for each of the above categories. Indeed, to perform Shakespeare today in Elizabethan dress (costume) might well be regarded as something of a radical 'interpretation'.

It is the director then who has come to interpret this historical repertory for a contemporary audience, and to integrate the various facets of production into a consistent style. The major element of production is still, of course, the actors, and it is in order to integrate the work of the actors into the complex of the production

that the director has come to have significant influence upon the
actors' work, and an interesting relationship has developed. However much the relationship is geared to and mediated by the
theatrical event, at a very basic level it will approximate the adult-
to-child relationship: the nurture and development of a being. As
suggested in the earlier section on actor psychology the director is
the adult assisting the actor/child in its rite of passage – rehearsal –
to the adult stage of personal freedom – performance – with the
sanction of approval/disapproval by the audience – the world at
large.

The dynamics of the actor–director relationship are influenced
by this pattern of growth. In the early rehearsal stage there is a
strong reliance – even if grudgingly – of the actor upon the director.
There is the need for nurturing and support; only the director
seems to know where any structure lies. The actor has yet to have
anything to hang on to, be it words, blocking or character. So the
actor needs to hold on to the director's hand, as the child clings
to the adult while taking its first stumbling steps. This, too, should
be the time for play; for exploration and discovery. Here the
director is guide, protector, creator of a safe environment, helper-
up of the fallen. He or she is also prescriber of parameters, both
in the limits of the space (where the actor can go) and the structure
of the text (whose life it is). At this stage the actor/child needs
attention, support, encouragement and positive control: which
translates practically into a nod, a glance, a smile, a touch, a
word.

'How did it feel?' is perhaps the most commonly asked question
in rehearsal. The mind, necessary at first for intellectual decoding
of the text, gradually gives over to the body and feeling. While
feeling out each other, actors also feel and test the space with
their bodies – taking armfuls and lungfuls of space, shrinking and
expanding themselves according to the dynamics of the action. 'It
felt right': when the fragments come together for a moment. Not
the struggling, juggling, tripping over tongue and feet in the early
rehearsals; now actors start to know in their bones that this is
what the character would do in these emotional and physical
circumstances. There comes a feeling of clarity and lightness, if
only for a moment; but once it is there it can come again and
expand to encompass the whole part. The actor is learning as a
child learns, by trial, error, osmosis and repetition. The character

starts to inhabit the actor; the body recognizes and fuses with it. Actors still know they are actors, that they are rehearsing, are consciously themselves; but gradually are being possessed by a creature recognized as growing from the energy of the playscript and sculpted together with fellow actors. When the process is complete, the actor can enter into the character's mask and take it off at will.

Just as the actor/child is exploring the limits of its ego demands with the director/adult in the social context of rehearsal ('I want'), so is the actor/character exploring the 'I want' of the character in the dramatic structure of the text. Both 'I want's encounter a structure to which an adaptation must take place. The director is there to facilitate these twin adaptations: to support the actor as a person so that the character created will fulfil the perceived needs of the play.

But before this metamorphosis to adult/character is achieved, there will come the trial by fire, for which the actor is never ready – the first run-through; stumble-through; stagger-through as it is fondly called, with wryly appropriate ambivalence. As if in tennis, the actor in recent rehearsals has been playing beautiful shots off the wall, off the ball-machine at his or her own pace – now, suddenly, the game is for real. The actor steps for the first time on to the unstoppable treadmill of action that is a performance. Everything happens much more quickly. Events start playing the actors and knock them staggering off the rhythm; they stumble over words and gestures that have not become instinctive parts of their characters; labour over actions that still need time for thought when now reaction is all there is time for. Then, suddenly, it is over – the end of the first run-through: relief if not quite triumph. It can be done!

On to performance. But, again, before this final stage is reached there is the potentially troublesome adolescent period of rehearsal development, when the actors have found their feet and seem to be less in need of support, and may even resent further guidance from the director. This apparent withdrawal can be a difficult time for both actors and director. The actor, in one sense, probably needs more support than ever as the approaching judgement by 'Them' – the audience, critics, the real world outside the safe environment of rehearsal – draws near. But the support is now of a different kind; the actor needs to start to believe 'it will work' but cannot yet trust his or her own judgement and only the director can be the touchstone. So it is a time of ambivalence. Actors need to withdraw, to cut the umbilical cord yet retain awareness that the director is there if needed. Some actors even seek criticism at this moment: it shows the director is still keeping an eye on their work. The line between giving the actors freedom without seeming to abandon them is very fine.

Probably one of the most delicate skills of the director–actor relationship is letting the actors go; giving them confidence and freedom to take the leap and run with it, while keeping a gentle hand on the reins of a performance so that the new-found power does not take it beyond the necessary disciplines of the craft and dynamics of the style. Actors invent, find impulses, feel rhythms in the body, solve problems on their feet. Directors suggest, restrain, select, shape, pace and phrase. Knowing when to give and when to take is at the heart of the successful rehearsal process.

'How do you learn all those lines?': the question most asked of the actor by the layman. There are probably two basic attitudes towards learning words, and in some respects they illustrate opposite poles of rehearsal approach. While all that has been said above is true and at some time is the experience of all actors in a rehearsal situation, the basic structure of rehearsals can differ significantly: whether words are learned by the actor before the rehearsal starts, or are learned during the rehearsal period, probably represents the polar opposites.

There is something to be said for each approach. The words are ciphers for the character's action, and the character's action contains its purposes and strategies. Until actors have made the words their own, the character cannot be completely created and assimilated. Some actors and directors like to 'get the words out of the way'. Actors learn the words before rehearsals begin, which relieves them of having to hold books. The rehearsal can proceed more smoothly and because words, action and character are so closely related, the character will start out well on its way to final form. Here, what the actor has to do in rehearsal is to make the words fit the structure of action that other actors and the director have developed.

This method does avoid some of the agonies of learning words during the rehearsal period. When actors are trying to remember words, they will not be open to the impulses of the action. It takes time for words to sink into the bones. A scene that was stone cold in the apartment the night before simply isn't there in the rehearsal room the next morning when cues are coming from all directions, feet are frozen to the floor, and nothing looks or sounds the same in the cold light of day.

All of this makes a positive case for 'getting the lines out of the way'. However, the danger is that a full exploration of the play goes with them. With the words an actor inevitably learns an approach to the action and begins to set character. Choices have to be made. So the rehearsal process becomes one of giving what you have got, adjusting to what you get, and glossing a smooth workable surface over the play.

As has been suggested, memory takes place in the body: just as we learn to speak, to walk, to ride a bicycle. To learn the lines in the context of discovering how the play works best recapitulates that organic process. To assimilate the words while exploring the text mutually with the director will create both more interesting choices for the play's action, and a deeper process of memorization for the actor. It will take longer. Messing around, making mistakes, finding impulses, allowing for surprises, rather than locking in choices with the first response to the words – in other words applying the childlike process of play to the rehearsal – does take time but can lead to more appropriate and interesting choices. In performance, the impulses of the scene will now play the actor. They will have arisen from interaction with fellow actors and physical responses from the text. Meaning will not have been imposed on words learned outside the total context of the evolving of the play from text to stage.

There is, of course, no one way, and time is always a factor, and often the enemy of the best results. Most actors bring their own process into rehearsal and serious problems only arise when quick-boilers and slow-simmerers, early memorizers and late evolvers cannot adapt to each other's process. Here is where the director, the mediator for the actors and probably the most important cybernetic affector and effector of the acting process, has to hold the ring and attempt to create a situation in which all actors can do their best work.

Interestingly, the polar opposites of memorization approximate to the polar opposites of directorial approaches. There are those directors who have all the moves written in their book before things start, and those who have a strong sense of where they are going, but are willing to proceed more loosely and take the actor into the process. Actors and directors have similar aims – getting the play to the stage – but different perspectives on the process. The director at some conscious level will be concerned for meaning. The actor's capacity to express meaning is not necessarily assisted by intellectual understanding. But the director, in a significant sense, determines what an actor is able to do; and just as in a child's life there are good Daddies and Mummies and bad Daddies and Mummies, so there are enabling directors and disabling directors. Ideally, a director will create an environment in which the actor can discover choices rather than be given them. A nurturer and facilitator, guide and possibly teacher who has done the homework, has a broad sense of where the production is going, and helps the actor move in that direction. A director who gives the actors freedom to explore and fail; who draws performance out of actors by neither spoon-feeding nor straitjacketing but by the kind of osmosis that informs an actor's work: to direct by indirection.

On the other hand, an actor will come across many kinds of disabling directors. These are usually authoritarian in some way; they perceive the actor purely as a sign rather than agent and enforce some preconception upon the production. The danger here is that not only will this stunt the actor's creation of the role but, as a child, the actor may be anxious not to displease and will give the director's performance against his or her own instincts. (Alas! The ever-present necessity to be rehired can reinforce this.) This kind of director's production can look tired very quickly and has nowhere to go when something isn't working. Coming from a vision that has not included the actor, it won't become deep-seated, can be brittle, hollow, and doesn't wear well. The disabling director may not even like actors, and his or her answer to 'Why don't they let actors act?' is probably, 'Where will you have the parrot, on the left shoulder or the right?'

Having said all this there are, of course, some brilliant authoritarian directors for whom actors are happy to work, carried along by the power of the director's imagination and the intensity of their energy. But actors soon sniff out directors who have neither imagination nor empathy.

Perhaps the most difficult directors for an actor to work with are the sociopsychologists, and the philosopher-critics. These can give brilliant studied disquisitions about a play, but may have no sense of how theatre operates at an instinctual or practical level. They are sometimes found in the ranks of the Academy where, at the final level, the academic mind deals in discourse. The director must finally deal in action.

However uncomfortable the marriage between actor and director can be, like divorce in modern society it is here to stay. The good director as nurturing, responsible, encouraging, demanding, playful adult is a positive force in the acting process; the guide in the rite of passage which takes the actor to performance and to that last link in the cybernetic loop of theatre – the audience.

Chapter 11

The cybernetics of acting: audience and critic

The cybernetical system which theatre sets up between playwright, director and actor is completed by the audience – the drama's patrons whom, as Johnson told us in *The Vanity of Human Wishes*, the actors must not only 'live to please' but 'please to live'. However interesting as a craft and fascinating as an ego experience, acting is finally done for an audience – the great 'Them', who for most actors are both enemy to be subdued and lover to be seduced; the impersonal personality that completes the performance; the many-headed Hydra that has to be made to listen and look in the actor's direction as if it were one. Joan Littlewood said there are no good or bad audiences, only good or bad performances. This may or may not be true, and many actors would disagree, but what is certainly true is that there are different audiences; and different audiences both evoke and require different responses from the actor.

At the simplest level, the audience on a wet Wednesday in Wigan is likely to be damper than on a sunny Saturday somewhere else. On a more political level, a young college audience with a pro-feminist sensibility is likely to be less amused by *The Taming of the Shrew* than is a Masonic lodge. (Neither is likely fully to appreciate Shakespeare's play!) Matinées particularly are days of dread for the actor – not just because of two performances on the same day, but because of the anticipated audiences. At one extreme, there are pensioners for whom the actors' main task is to keep them awake, and on the other hand school matinées when the actors often wish the audience could be put to sleep. The actor and writer Simon Brett, in his *What Bloody Man is That?*[1] is instructive on these latter. A group of provincial repertory actors, performing *Macbeth* for a school audience, are discussing which lines are likely to get the most response. They bet that 'and some I see/That two-fold balls and treble sceptres carry' will break up the audience just ahead of 'I have given suck'. They are, of course, right![2]

If school matinées may be thought of as too much audience participation of a more sexual than textual nature, the question of the way in which much audience participation is determined today can, at a very fundamental level, be related to the spatial dynamics of the actor–audience relationship. For example, the actor on a traditional Shakespearean stage is able to relate directly to the audience and bring it into the action, making it participate in a way that is not available to the actor on the proscenium stage with its peephole space. Locked in a darkened room, with the sense of looking in on its neighbour, the proscenium audience's basic response will tend to be in terms of 'how lifelike', and judgement of the actor's work will be in the perspective of what might appropriately take place in a contemporary living room.

This response has been compounded by the pervasiveness of the highly unresponsive form of television, in which the audience is not asked for input and the actor knows to expect none. It is instructive that actors on a set like response from the crew and other actors – the camera is a dull audience. Actors don't really want to act for themselves. Theatre is a social act, a ritual of communion, a 'palace of virtuosities'; and a game that two sides have to play for it to work.

Just as the experiments with space in recent years have been aimed at returning theatre to a tradition of more open relationships between actor, text and audience, so the work of many post-realist playwrights and directors has moved towards penetrating the fourth wall and crossing the 'mystic gulf': Beckett, by an all-embracing mixture of existential metaphors with popular devices; Brecht, by requiring the audience to participate, at least on a cerebral level, in his dialectic; Artaud, by his attempt to include both actor and audience in an enveloping sensual experience. This has created problems for some actors who had become used to working within themselves, and for audiences who had become used to a passive form of what Brecht would call 'culinary' response.

Are there any basic dynamics of the actor–audience relationship

or is it all a question of understanding and accommodating to
particular conventions at a particular moment: reading the 'sign'
of the times, as it were? All of which brings us to the question of
what constitutes an audience's response. Indeed, an important
issue for contemporary criticism is what constitutes an 'audience'
and informs its perception.

We are a long way from the idea of communion that created
the community of Greek and Shakespearean audiences: visible and
palpable to the actor, sharing common daylight, weather, life. The
audience was then an actor in the joint theatrical venture; the
play, as both ceremony and metaphor, was a unifying element of
the communal sensibility. Today, not only have actor and audience
been subject to the technically divisive influence of the fourth
wall and the darkened auditorium, but the equally divisive social
influence of industrial capitalist, product-oriented specialization, of
which theatre has become a part.

One of the questions that exercises proponents of the new hist-
oricism is 'What *is* an audience, and how may we judge what it
perceives?' This issue is not too far removed from the phenomenological one concerning the actor–character relationship, but it has
a more specifically social and political bent. An audience is seen
as a body of thought and desire: the victim of its own history. Its
perception, its 'gaze', will be tainted by its desire both to see the
theatrical product in the way in which it has been taught to
perceive by the social, political and economic circumstances which
historically have formed its sensibility, and also to consume the
product as any other comestible item of a capitalist economic
structure. This is what Brecht was speaking of in his idea of
'culinary' narcotic theatre, in which actor and audience give each
other what is necessary in order to sustain each other in the system
within which they are trapped: a mutual sustenance and a mutual
domination. This is clearly a perspective which cannot be ignored
in speaking today of the relationship between actor and audience,
as it will inform the perception and reception of any performance
in a particular situation.

Significant as this issue is, it is perhaps more for the critic and
director than for the actor, who, in practical terms, works in the
moment and will respond for better or for worse to the immediate
positive or negative input from the audience. However corrupted
in sociopolitical character, and however disparate and alienated in

existential terms the contemporary audience may be, the actor, when working, perceives it as a corporate body and plays to this. This will occur even though the audience may be nothing more than united in its divisions, in seeking the communion, the social identity it feels lacking elsewhere, and which it hopes through this ceremony of theatre to achieve; if only for that time. Also, however negatively perceived in political terms the idea of the tainted gaze may be, it is possible that a mutuality of desire is a point of reciprocity or audience and actor: a practical connection in the moment.

Here one is reminded of the myth of Prometheus. The audience (spell)bound to its seat, as Prometheus was chained to his rock, is constrained to watch: given the self-consciousness to be aware of its condition without the ability to comprehend. With a gaze that can never know what it is to 'know'; desiring to understand the irredeemable condition – while the actor pecks at its liver. The actors, equally desiring to feed their own uncertainty, their vulnerability, their need. A similar, if more sentimental image, would be the Christian one of the pelican feeding its young from its breast. Actor and audience both have a desire for survival; though neither understands the purpose. The desire for and lack of knowledge unites actor and audience. It is the actor's part to desire and be desired, playing out the half-remembered and half-understood vision of a sacred yet blasphemous eternity. It is the audience's part to consume and be consumed, by the acting out of its own darkest fears and aspirations.

The relationship, at bottom, is still the original one: desire for the communion that is no longer present in our post-modern condition; a desire for belonging, as the audience members sit isolated in their darkness. If they become for a while only a congregation of private moments shared with the actor – albeit comestibly through desire, possession – it may be enough. For, with the desire for communion goes still the desire for understanding of self: 'Who's there? Nay answer me.'[3] Failing answers, there is the satisfaction of the desire for immediate, if unsatisfactory possession: I am looking at you, looking at me, looking at you. Both actor and audience need reassurance of their existence from the other's presence – however uncertain, corrupt and tainted that present gaze may be said to be. But tainted from whose point of view? The critical conundrum comes full circle and joins with the uncertain question of the audience's perspective: who's looking at whom, from where, and with what eye? Although forewarned long ago by the Watchman in the *Oresteia*, and the self-blinding of Oedipus, it may have taken us until now – the late twentieth century – to be fully aware of the uncertainty yet dreadful brutality of sight, of any gaze. To pass the time pleasurably in the gap of the question may be the best we can hope for.

Pleasurably. As Brecht observed, indeed, instinctively approved, it is probably fair to say that an audience goes to the theatre primarily to experience. The audience's basic response is likely to be in terms of enjoyment rather than analysis. Was it a pleasurable, entertaining experience? Did they have a good time? As Theseus asks in *A Midsummer Night's Dream*, 'Is there no play/To ease the anguish of a torturing hour?' (Act V, Scene i). A play to pass the time pleasurably with expectation of gratification at different levels, from the simple titillation of farce to a richly layered drama. But at whatever levels, first and foremost pleasurably; and audience enjoyment, or otherwise, is palpable to the actor on stage.

Thus, 'How good was the acting?' is probably not the first question an audience asks itself. The critic may consciously ask this; other actors in the audience may be aware of it; the more sophisticated spectators may ask this after the event. But in the moment, the audience tends to suspend its judgement with its disbelief. A popular audience will normally have no difficulty in accepting the 'tainted' magic of theatre. An innocent 'lay' audience can receive the full effect of the play, giving itself up to it and being absorbed in its fabric, in a way that the critically sophisticated – concerned for understanding more than appreciation – may not. If the story line is clear and interesting, the audience will gladly accept what the critic or academic might regard as appalling inconsistencies of convention and style. If the audience is given enough information, and the actors believe in what they are giving, then an audience will tend to believe what it is asked to believe.

The actor has always to let the audience know the part it is expected to play in the event. If the play is funny, the actor has to give the audience licence to laugh. Thus, while it isn't necessary for an audience to be aware of a play's style, i.e. the way in which it is intended to take living form, it is necessary for the actor to be aware of this in order to share the playing with the audience by showing it the rules of the game. An audience will feel somewhat off-kilter when it isn't brought into the play by the actors; when, however corrupted, its desire isn't being fulfilled. The audience doesn't have to understand conventions to be aware of this; it doesn't have to be able to discuss details of the acting; it doesn't even have to be self-conscious of its gaze; it will just feel there is something wrong – it isn't having a good time.

Perhaps one touchstone of acting is how far it fulfils and illuminates the demands of the play's action and style. Perhaps 'good' acting must be able to communicate this in such a way as to engage the audience. 'Perhaps' is repeated here because there will never be more than a range of possible answers; there will always be many levels of possible judgements and contradictions among these.

If the modern, democratic audience may be said to be a disparate group of uncertainly influenced individuals, the professional critic seems to be endowed with all the authority of the Sovereign in the court theatres of the seventeenth and eighteenth centuries. If perhaps not now the focal point of view of every gaze, the critic is frequently the fickle point of view behind it. A complete discussion of the tendentious issue of criticism, as that of what constitutes an 'informed' audience, goes far beyond the bounds of this book, but both will have a significant influence upon the actor's career. If the actor has an ambivalent relationship with the audience, the actor's view of the critic probably depends upon the nature of any review. Though many actors pretend not to read notices, and some actually manage not to, it is the lucky actor who can treat the 'two imposters' of praise and blame equally, secure in his or her ability. Which is, of course, what the actor who is to survive must do, concerned for the arc of the career rather than the ephemeral moments of triumph or disaster.

Criticism can be valuable, and actors aren't always the best judges of their own work. But critics will have their own gaze, their own agendas: to establish their own careers; to sell newspapers. Even the best of criticism does tend to come at the most vulnerable time for the actor – the opening night, when the trepidation of meeting an audience for the first time is compounded by the knowledge that it is on this one shot that posterity is going to find the written judgement of the work. There is the further issue of whether an actor can, or even should, adjust performance to criticism. An actor is part of an ensemble, and the balance of the production and the work of fellow actors depends upon playing the part as agreed in rehearsal – for better or worse. Then again it is your performance, not the critic's. What do they know? Simon Callow speaks for all actors in his litany of an actor's response to criticism:

> the critic doesn't know shit,
> but suppose he or she is right,
> the part is badly written,
> I got no/bad direction,
> I wonder if I'll work again,
> Drinking.[4]

The very worst kind of criticism is that written for the critic's ego as an essay in dismissively clever language with no positive consciousness of the actor, who has to continue to go out there and put him- or herself on the line. Such criticism can be personally destructive – like telling Christ that the crucifixion didn't work, but has to be done again six times a week with two matinées.

The final issue between actor and critic is a fundamental difference in approach. It is instinct versus intellect. Actors work instinctively and in the moment; and, finally, so does an audience: a performance is more absorbed than understood. Through the obfuscating scrim of phenomenological perception and political coloration, and despite the many possible levels of appreciation and judgement, there will be at any one performance a community of response that is created by the symbiosis of play. The disparate elements, the many heads of the audience, became one for the occasion. Just as the actor speaks to, both literally and figuratively, the middle of the audience, so the audience median speaks back, or rather responds, through the invisible but palpable umbilical cord that ties actor and audience together in their mutual desire to celebrate in all its joys and sorrows their joint connection with life itself.

This sense of an entity, of a many-faceted being, enables the actor in performance to 'play' the audience in a one-to-one confrontation. The audience is perceived as a felt presence which it is possible to control or influence through skills. A comedy presents the most obvious concrete response for the actor with the immediate judgement of laughter; and even a smile creates a tangible warmth. The comedic rhythm established with an audience allows the actor to time the laughs for better effect, holding back the punch-line or word to get a bigger release of pent-up expectation; or riding quickly over minor laughs to point the major moment. At the other end of the spectrum, tragedy, a less collaborative form, makes itself equally felt in the absolute stillness and silence of the audience; as it is confronted with the solitude of its own destiny, fed by the actor's sacrifice.

So, accepting all the possible givens – different plays with different conventions; different places with different spaces; different gazes with different desires; and the imponderables of the hierarchy of response, sophisticated or simple (for example, the apocryphal dentist whose response to *Romeo and Juliet* was that Juliet needed orthodontic treatment) – finally, the multitude of signs emitted by a performance will coalesce into a general impression received by the actors. For the actors, it is a one-to-one situation, us with and against the great Them who have come to see the sideshow: Them thirsting for entertainment and sacrifice. The actor first hears the beast roaring to itself over the tannoy in the dressing room. Do they sound tractable? 'How are they?' is the question asked of those who make the first entrance; will it be thumbs up or thumbs down? In the dressing room the actors gird up their loins for the confrontation and the feast; go through personal rituals that quell the demons and bring luck.

Performance is an aggressive/erotic experience. 'Knock 'em dead', 'Fuck 'em', 'Lay them in the aisles'. The language of the confrontation reveals this. The adversarial posture produces the necessary energy while the fact that it is play controls the danger, as animals at play sheath their claws. The audience, while satisfying its desire by devouring the actor with its eyes – the 'gaze' which is such an issue for current critical 'perception' – also feeds the actor. Not only in simple technical ways of letting the actor know in performance whether the narrative is clear, the timing right, how a moment should be played, but in the seductiveness of its approval, its embrace. While it consumes the actor with its eyes, ears, heart, mind and groin, sustenance from the audience enables the actor to continue in a career that by most of its auguries shouldn't exist. Yes, the mutual desire can be corrupting. Yes, the actor desensitized by the need to make a career on the capitalist production belt can learn simply to give the audience what it wants. Yes, the audience, while knowing it is being seduced, still wants to believe it is satisfying its own desire. Sometimes it is necessary for survival that there should be less than meets the eye. But somehow, with the ambivalence of the child that desires acceptance but refuses to compromise with the adult world, the actor in front of the audience, while needing to be embraced and taken in, manages to preserve the residual independence of an atavistic force. To retain the objectivity to mirror society's shortcomings – as well as its virtues – to itself: to remain a dangerous outsider, while being a sacrifice for the general good.

Chapter 12

Acting as danger and sacrifice

That acting has, throughout its history, been regarded as a threat to civilized society, and the actor regarded, both in terms of function and lifestyle, as a social outsider, is well testified by historical account and anecdote. Plato regarded actors as hypocrites, parlayers of illusion and falsifiers of truth. He feared that the mask they wore would become their faces and be a threat to his Republic. In Rome, the Justinian code stated that anyone who appeared on stage was marked with infamy. Actors were deprived of the rights of citizenship and often flogged for the good of their souls. Elizabethan actors were either servants of the nobility or lumped together with vagabonds and sturdy beggars who could be whipped from the parish boundaries.

The sensibility of the romantic period didn't help. The idea of the artist as loner, outside society's corrupting forces, was applied to the actor, but without the exclusion of corruption. As Rousseau said, 'The actor must be possessed of reckless enthusiasm incompatible with a settled life and financial security.' He thought that 'disrespect is in the nature of the profession; counterfeiting himself; being passionate in cold blood. Putting his person publicly on sale.'[1]

This idea of prostitution was equally present in the Victorian period, when it was customary for whores picked up by the police to describe themselves as actresses: the Soho 'model' is today's equivalent. At Kean's trial for cuckolding Alderman Cox, the *London Times* thundered, 'It is of little consequence whether Richard or Othello be well acted; it is important that public decency be not outraged.'[2] Prosecuting counsel also described Kean as

'Your client, bred to tumble for his meat/To act the monkey in plebian street.'[3]

While the Victorian period provided Dickens with the 'host of shabby, poverty stricken men' referred to in the *Pickwick Papers*, it did begin the bourgeois acceptance and adulation of the star: Irving was the first actor to be knighted. But the general view of the actor, held even by those who would at times acknowledge a particular worth, was expressed by Dirk Bogarde quoting his father, in his memoir, that it was a 'lunatic, mediocre, ungentlemanly career'.[4] To this day, as Charlton Heston has put it,[5] actors will likely seduce your wife, your daughter, even worse be homosexual, drink, won't wash and don't pay their bills. Ironically amusing enough, the Screen Actors' Guild won't take a personal cheque from an actor in payment of admission fees – it has to be a cashier's cheque. Even actors don't trust actors.

In fact, actors *do* trust actors; sort of. There is a community of the beyond-the-pale; a gallows humour of those who have to hang together or will hang separately. Part of the codependence of those who have survived and who 'know'; who are playing a joke on life that at any minute might backfire. Of those who can never dare to hope too much; who have to stand tall and assert their place in full public view, but always have a small feeling that their fly may be undone. Who fear that it all may be an illusion, a house of cards and that Them, the audience, the representatives of 'normal' society, will find them guilty of the unspeakable crime of pretending to be actors. So, the deliberate campness or gallows humour of the dressing room. 'Oh God, I've already peaked.' 'I'm falling out of caricature; I'd better put on more makeup.' 'I hate working with rank professionals.' All of this to keep up the pretence that it isn't serious; to laugh at the fact that it's no job for a grown-up person; to keep one's sanity against the dangerous, courageous, and terrific act of standing on the earth and trying to mean something.

It is the danger present in acting that leads society to keep the actor in the outsider's place. The danger has a twofold response from society: an attraction and a repulsion. The actor in many ways is licensed to do what many members of society have an itch to do but know the safety of society would be destroyed if they were allowed similar licence. The actor, in putting on other faces, is embodying other souls and the Christian tradition tells us that only Satan does this. In one sense the actor is a permanent Vice figure! Attractive and repelling, entertaining but dangerous; representing the Devil, or at least villainy, and villainy is attractive at its level of freedom. Villainy is energy and cleverness. It can be revitalizing and seductive compared with paradise with its boring potential of unlimited honey, harp music and bland, beatific smiles. The actor gives us a thrill by releasing our repressed energies for us; but, like Jack-in-the-box, we need to know he can be shut back into the box at any moment.

The attractiveness of the actor has something to do with the energy needed to overcome danger, which invests the actor with power. In a very personal sense the actor 'risks the stage', and risk excites the audience. Part of the applause is for the success of the actor at passing through the potential pitfalls of the role. The audience wants the actor to succeed, it needs to feel that risks can be successfully taken in life – life itself being the ultimate risk. But at the same time there is the hope of proving the actor mortal, no better than them; why you and not me! Actors must be made to prove their talent and justify the enormity of their willingness to stand there and reveal themselves before the weight of everyone's eye. The risk for the actor is that of being seen as naked beneath audience gaze; not only failing in terms of talent/power to prove one's right to be there, but in very simple terms to miss an entrance, to miss a cue, to drop a line which, suddenly, in the awful existential vacuum of silence that follows, reveals the actor beneath the mask, with no reason to be there and nothing to define his or her existence. It is in one sense a form of death, or at least the suspension of being; just as breaking into laughter inappropriately on stage is known as 'corpsing' in the British theatre – the mask of character is dropped and the character has temporarily died.

With nothing but a film of makeup between themselves and both the audience and their own eternity, it is a courageous and dangerous act to say, 'Look at me. Listen to me. I have something to say.' The ability to do this lies in the dimensionality of an actor's talent: a word that has been implied but kept away from so far in this discussion. Like 'presence' and other abstruse terms applied to acting, the intractable problem of the meaning of 'talent' makes pale the earlier problems of dealing with the seemingly concrete part of acting – the sign. Presence, as the word suggests, has to do with being totally present in the moment – we spend much of our time as human beings living in the past or future. The actor fills the moment, and his or her energy radiates out into space to draw in the audience with the power of the magnetic field set up. The actor is a transformer, plugged into the energy of the universe, capturing and transforming that lightning into communicative energy. The more kilowatts per instant the actor can radiate, the more will be his or her power in the moment and the stronger the presence.

In process dynamics, this power is related to the strength of the need, the desire, the 'I want', in both actor and character terms. The investment of energy in gaining the objective – wanting harder than anyone else – draws out and channels the power and gives interest in the smallest stage moment. It also adds vulnerability, because the more you want, the greater the risk of failure. This interaction of power and vulnerability sets up a field of force in the actor, creates a perception that the actor may explode at any moment. All 'great' actors have this power, this sense that an explosion might take place and that those of us watching will be covered with human tripe. This potential also lends a constant sense of the unexpected, the possible release of spontaneous 'uncontrolled' reactions, no matter how controlled the performance is. One of the great abilities of the skilful actor is not to let skill, technique, get in the way of this outburst of the unexpected; but at the same time to keep it contained within the bounds of the performance, thus heightening its power.

This energy, this life force which the actor brings to performance, is partly rooted in sexual energy and owes some of its chemical attraction to that. There is an animal quality about powerful acting. There is an omnivorous voraciousness about it, a territoriality that claims all space and consumes all within its reach. And the consumption, the voraciousness, contains a power sexually to disturb, to attract, to seduce. We need only look at the evidence of one of the earliest of western dramas, Euripides' *The Bacchae*, to know the seductive and destructive power of the Dionysian creative force. This passionate id is one of the roots of the power and the presence of the actor.

It is now clearer why the actor is an outsider in society. The actor revives and incorporates in the work that creative spark which underlies the nature of things, but whose terrific power is also capable of subverting the order that society has carved so painfully out of the original, powerful chaos of the Big Bang. In order to protect itself from itself, from the destructive and chaotic side of the Dionysian potential, 'normal' members of society have had to give up much of the force of libido, to restrain themselves from dwelling on much of the rest, and to wear only those masks that society has scrutinized, sanitized, authorized, legalized.

It is part of the actor's task to tear off the calcified mask of social lies, politeness and good taste, and to reveal the dark and dynamic underbelly of society to itself. As with Yeats (*The Circus Animals' Desertion*, III), the actor must:

Lie down where all the ladders start
In the foul rag-and-bone shop of the heart.

This is a necessary task if society is not to be suffocated under the weight of its own hypocrisies, but it is a threatening task which has been left to the actor, who is metaphorically and often literally caged behind the fourth wall of the stage. The audience acclaims the actor from its safe remove. It is amazed or amused to see the otherness it only dreams or fantasizes about performed on the stage. It applauds the risk it itself is not allowed to take; it wants to flirt with danger but equally wants to be affirmed in its own probity, and be able to dismiss the actor from its daily thoughts. So the actor is held in contempt for using the licence granted to him; and is ironically called a hypocrite for dealing at a remove with society's own hypocrisies.

It is this risk, the constant self-sacrifice for a society that alternately embraces and rejects, which produces in the theatre geniuses and drunks, and not infrequently both at the same time. This finally insupportable responsibility of performing the constantly heroic act; both in simply facing the audience, and taking on its sins and its hopes. It is this tension which lends force to acting, but which can destroy actors.

The 'piss-artist' is a not uncommon type in the acting profession, and at a very basic level the resort to liquor as both stimulant and soporific is an understandable function of the risk and the 'high' of performance. The need for fuel and Dutch courage before the event. The need to unwind, to release the tremendous pent-up energy after the event, produces the classic conviviality of actors in a bar at one o'clock in the morning. And the everyday solitariness, the waiting of not being in work, can all too easily be filled by the ephemeral fellowship of the pub, and the blurry oblivion of the bar. Then there are those who simply believe they act better on Chivas Regal. But there is a deeper, time-honoured tradition for the release of truth *in vino veritas*: the Dionysian creative ecstasy being produced by wine. Wine and poetry, wine and inspiration; actors have to put the unspeakable mystery into words, they have to speak with tongues; as a German lawyer pleading on behalf of an actor has said: 'Actors are not normal people; sex and alcohol play a great part in their lives.'[6]

The actor is not 'normal': he has been given, and needs to sustain the place as an outsider. For this, stimulus and support are necessary, both to reveal and anaesthetize the vulnerability, to touch ecstasy and to ease its pain. Ironically, although they constantly create a world of illusion, actors cannot escape from the reality of the world. They are always conscious of the fact that we are all food for worms. Alas, poor Yorick! Yet they are charged with keeping vitality in life by flirting with – be it as tragic hero or comic clown – the dangerous presence of death within life. For this the actor needs courage; if at times from a bottle.

We have said that actors don't train like dancers and singers. But in one sense, actors, being their own instruments, are in training all the time, as they absorb or suck in experience. On stage, it is not the ordinary that is dramatic, exciting or illuminates ordinary experience. It is possible that actors may have to touch the 'dissolute' as well as the sublime in order to tune their instrument to the full. Simon Callow has spoken of his mentor, Micheál Mac Liammóir, as bedizened, berouged and blasphemous, fuelled by gin and tea.[7] Mac Liammóir was a great actor and a Celt. Many great actors have been drunks; many of them Celts. Perhaps here the Dionysian tradition, the bardic tradition, and the tradition of the social and political outsider come together in the myth that spans ages of the dissolute renegade creative outsider.

Here I will admit an enormous leap of intuition, but it seems not coincidental that the contradiction between the freedom demanded by the poetic soul and the entrapment occasioned by political restriction may produce in the Celtic consciousness an ecstasy and an *Angst* that require libations both to propitiate Dionysus and to induce Lethe. To extrapolate further, the necessary licence to embark upon flights of fancy and acts of anarchy, neither of which are containable within normal bourgeois society, tends to produce in many actors an instinctive leftishness in politics: as outsiders they are on the side of outsiders everywhere.

As has been suggested, part of this position is a necessary choice if the actor is not to get locked into rigid and specific ways of seeing and viewing the world. Thus, in very practical terms, if the actor is not to limit the possible range of the emotional palette, expressed in choices of character and action, he or she must keep open, flexible, and not be restricted by or to any particular sociopolitical structure. This necessary liberation of self will tend to put the actor on the side of liberalism in life: feeling, immediacy, anti-authoritarianism, pro-people rather than politician; pro-gypsy rather than government. The actor defiantly wears the baton-sinister of society's bastard love child.

Danger comes with this territory. The danger to society is equalled by the dangers of existing outside society. The sacrament of self-expression carries the sanction of self-destruction. Cast with us out of paradise, the actor is at the forefront of the eternal quest for answers. The quest that ends in death. The actor knows both too much and too little; has a glimpse of the mystery that is out of reach. Charged with carrying the insupportable burden the priest has resigned, the actor must remain vulnerable to ultimate feeling while needing to deaden its pain. It is small wonder that the actor, denied the wine of bourgeois sacraments, has sometimes recourse to other less religiously sanctioned stimulants: both to induce and endure a deeper religiosity.

Despite the original connection between acting and religious ritual, the established church, as moral arbiter for society, has been one of the actor's main enemies. While the original religious mysteries dealt with all of life, accepting and recognizing the value of its potentially destructive energies, the priests of the church wanted to whip this devil out of humankind, to sublimate the erotic and turn the human voraciousness for total experience into the mosaic litany of shalt nots. It has been left to the poet and his significator the actor, the guardians of the half-remembered myths and stories of humankind, to point to what was missing and to reveal the hypocrisy behind the established 'truths'.

Patently, this is dangerous to the upholders of social morality. It must be acknowledged that actors, while preserving their place as outsiders, have not infrequently had to accommodate the dangerous truths of acting to the received ethos of society in order to exist at all. John Whiting has said that the purpose of art is to raise doubt while the purpose of entertainment is to reassure. The purpose of acting will always be to entertain, in the truest sense of the word: to come amongst with a purpose to engage the being. However, certainly since the eighteenth century when theatre became a part of bourgeois society, entertainment has come to have the sense of blandly passing away time, and in this context acting can become the use of empty and superficial masks to cover a hollowness of content. Here the mask will have a simplistic, titillating value. It is, indeed, reassuring society that its comfortable values are right and will not be disturbed.

It is possibly here that the, finally invalid, dichotomy between 'technical' actors and 'honest' actors grew up. Even when the mask is empty it has to be supported by a technique of performance in order to communicate at all – however facilely. What we have here is the actor playing the memory of a memory or the sign of a sign. All too often there is an attempt to substitute charm for content, to reassure the audience that the actor is harmless and on their side. Such facileness, however, does not belong to 'technical' actors alone; it can also be a function of 'honest' acting. This can become a self-serving display of the actor's personal emotion or psyche, what has been described by Michael Malone as 'glamorizing the neuroses of the artist into a signature of the seriousness of the art.'[8] Which has equally no connection with Whiting's sense of art. Neither 'charming' nor 'honest' performance raises doubt – one raises a sycophantic smile, the other sanctimonious sweat. In neither instance is there real danger or true sacrifice: in neither instance is the God present.

The mask, in the true sense in which it has been used throughout this essay, derives from the earliest rites and rituals of tribal societies, and is connected to and informed by the sacrificial spirit of these events. The wearer of the mask in humanity's earliest displays of mimetic celebration of existence was the shaman. The shaman is the forerunner of the priest, but a significant difference, both in the nature of the rites and the function of the shaman, is the holistic nature of the tribal celebration – the spirits were sacred but not sanitized.

The rites over which the shaman presided were concerned with the great events of human existence: puberty rites and the initiation of the young men into the tribe; fertility rites propitiating the gods for the fruitfulness of both land and the women of the tribe; dances for the successful hunting rites of the tribe, and to dramatize the stories of these successes. All of this is connected both to the very life spirit of the tribe (a recital of its identity) and to the roots of our own dramatic forms. We are storytelling animals and cannot bear to suffer, undramatized, daily events that define our fortunes both here and in the unknown world of otherness. These early rites over which the shaman presided were holistic in the sense that there was no distance between performer and spectator, it was a celebration that involved all. They were equally holistic in the sense that they celebrated every part of the tribe's existence. Sexuality and death were approached reverently as equal parts of the central mystery of life. They were confronted and worshipped, not regarded as evils to be covered with a fig-leaf or lulled comfortably into a better world to come by the priest.

The priest, pontifex – maker of bridges between the gods and the audience – is our gentrified descendant of the shaman, as both performer and celebrator of the sacred rites. One of the fortuitously metaphorical stories that theatre throws up concerns Laurence Olivier, who thought he was going to follow his brother to India as a civil servant, only to be told by his father, a priest, 'You are going on the stage.' It would be nice to imagine the traces of a tribal memory or spirit, which led the father to encourage his son to continue on the journey both had commenced with the shaman: the original mask wearer, who enacted out as both totemic sign and spiritual metaphor the great forces of tribal life which the mask invoked, and whose spirits possessed the wearer.

The roots of acting lie in that atavistic magical possession and sharing of the spirit. In all great acting, possession of a sort takes place. The vitality and power of the actor lie in the potential danger as well as the healing power of the matter with which he or she deals. By facing him or herself, the actor faces the world, and through the sacrifice of crucifixion attempts to achieve redemption for all. G.K. Chesterson has said that at the back of our minds we have a forgotten blaze, a burst of astonishment at our own existence. The actor has the power to bring this to the forefront of our lives if only for an instant. The actor encapsulates the *mana* of society, helps us touch the mystery of that intuitive, imaginal world which is deadened and buried under the routine of the everyday reality.

In tribal societies, the shaman identifies himself when quite young by his capacity for trance and possession of spirits; by his essential connection with 'otherness', being transported by the spirits of the other reality, and using this power for the health of the tribe. So, too, the actor as interpreter of humankind to itself must stand outside of society as well as be a member of it; must oblige the audience to face the most secret part of themselves, that which lies in the atavistic world of myth and spirit.

To reach an accommodation between this world and the reality of twentieth-, soon to be the twenty-first-century life, the actor assumes whatever mask of the time is demanded by the performance. The mask reflects the dominant image of humankind in any era. This may be the sacrifice and assumption of an Oedipus or a Hamlet; the absent core of self of a Peer Gynt; or the circular existential stasis of a Didi and Gogo. The necessary mask is a sign of the time, but will be a metaphor for eternity.

A society's deepest concerns are 'implicated in the nature of its heroic dramatic enterprises'; they are focused by the actor and purged by the sacred and blasphemous freedom he or she inherits. An actor is powerful and dangerous because of connection with otherness, the world we can never quite identify, but constantly feel is threatening to undermine us: Kafka's knock on the door at four in the morning; Osborne's sense that 'today's the day they'll find me out'. The actor leaps the ontological split – daring in both exposure and aspiration.

The state of possession is made manifest in the sign. Just as the shaman in an elevated spiritual state uses rhythmically articulated signs, so with the actor's gestures; and the distance of the actor in the frame surrounding the sign gives it a clarity, intensity and power in excess of that in the 'real' world. Actors define themselves in terms of such supra reality: otherness. They are 'shadows' such stuff as dreams are made of, and the power and danger of the act exerts a strong attraction upon the rest of us.

The actor's self-definition is a journey taken upon our behalf. Acting is, in one sense, always a journey undertaken by the actor in search of the self. The self-revelation of the actor requires casting off the superficial mask of accepted social propriety or shallow entertainment, and the discovery of the spiritual mask which may be in touch with excess, profanation, sacrilege: the tearing away of the false masks by the discovery of the true.

The actor pursues the dangerous steps to selfhood through the performance. The intensity of the enquiry and self-revelation engages the audience in a similar journey of self-enquiry and self-realization; and hopefully it is assisted in finding that understanding of its own self and purposes, which it is constantly struggling in its 'real' life to do. Standing inside itself, the human being always has a sense of possession by an intangible otherness, but is denied an objectivity, a clarity of self, which the actor in his or her conscious duality is trying to define. In some sense the actors' phenomenological dividedness allows them to bridge the ontological gap.

By definition, the rite of passage, quest, journey to the discovery of the self must end in death. Death is the final sanction of life. When we become aware of self we are immediately aware of separation from the mother and the uncertainty and fear of the otherness of the world. The cutting of the umbilical cord which launches us on our journey towards death is constantly with us. The search for self-identity is our attempt to come to terms with this, but it is always bound up with uncertainty, fear and final knowledge of death. Play is one way in which we test the world, create ourselves and find its reaction to us. The sanctioned and formalized players, the actors, face their destiny at each opening. They get to die many different deaths; but because they are sanctioned deaths, they are performed in the safety of the knowledge that they will be resurrected at the end of the performance. The actors bow to our acknowledgment of the trials they have endured on our behalf, and then rise from the bow, a resurrection, a sign which sends us, possibly purged, but hopefully reaffirmed, upon our way.

Wherever and whenever the actor takes the journey, its attraction will lie in its danger: will the journey end in death? What trials and tribulations will be met on the quest? How heroically will they be met? The journey encompasses the essential spiritual mystery, the sacrifice of acting. The act of acting is a sharing of the self, the channelling of the mystery, the expiation of the unspeakable sin of living, and redemption by willingness to face life totally: as creation, procreation and death. The actor is saying to the audience: 'Watch me being cut up. Watch my guts being spilled. Take this piece of me, of my flesh and blood. I hope you find it nourishing and illuminating, for I am your double and it is also a piece of yourself. Through the character you are getting me, and the character is yourself.'

The connection here, both with the original tribal ritual sacrifice of hero and scapegoat and with the Christian Mass, is not lost. The dichotomous, Janus-like situation of the actor as both social outsider/scapegoat and self-sacrificial redeemer, encompasses and parallels society's oldest myths. The actor still attempts to redeem mystery in a materialistic, scientific world: wearing the many masks of our sophistic(ated) society, the actor attempts to revive and reveal the lost myths of our atavistic soul. As John Guare has said: 'it is an attempt to insure that the original crime is never forgotten, the original wound never goes away, is always about to be performed, and is always in the present tense'.[9] It is as Shakespeare told us a 'monstrous' act: 'What's Hecuba to him or he to Hecuba?'[10] The actor is everything and nothing. Shakespeare understood the phenomenological dichotomy long ago. And the ultimate dichotomy is sacrifice: death to ensure the continuance of life. Acting, as sign and sacrifice, is finally an attempt to illuminate, if not resolve, the paradox of life itself.

Coda

It was suggested at the beginning of this discussion that it was not the author's intention to find an answer. But if there is anything that seems to be a common thread in exploring the idea of acting it is, ironically, the notion of dichotomy and paradox. Throughout the written history and criticism of acting, the actor tends to be spoken of in opposing terms. Without redundantly recapitulating the earlier argument in all its particulars, it is instructive that dichotomies, dualities, antinomies have cropped up in every aspect of the discussion. Diderot's title, *Le Paradoxe sur le comédien*,[1] with Archer's *Masks or Faces*,[2] probably represent the most evident examples of this ambiguity, and seem to bring us back to where we came in.

The very starting point of this discussion of acting was the phenomenological problem of the actor as both mask and face, self and character at the same time. We then saw that the semioticians' efforts were primarily aimed at doing away with ambivalence and creating a precise vocabulary to describe the act of performance. One of the weaknesses found in the semioticians' attempts was the metaphorical potential of the sign. What we may now call the otherness, the incorporeality it represents – as well as the corporeal human self.

Reviewing further, the actor, in psychological terms, was suggested to be in a state of controlled schizophrenia. Mythologically, the mark of Cain or kiss of Calliope was invoked. In the realm of religion, acting was perceived as both sacred and blasphemous; affirming and transgressing society's attempt to maintain a moral order. The Dionysian spirit, one of the catalysing dynamics of the dramatic act, is both ecstatically creative and demonically destructive. The actor is the subject of both society's adulation and revulsion. One could go on.

Doubling is found in the very structure of dramatic form. This technique underlines, in the use of mistaken identity, the uncertainty we have about ourselves in our lives, and the divided pulls of social form and instinctive desires – super-egos and ids – with which the actor deals. One of the more famous examples of double identity is Jack Worthing in *The Importance of Being Earnest*, who was Ernest in town and Jack in the country: a double life which allowed the worthy(ing) JP to keep up social face while letting down libidinous hair.

We have suggested it to have been the actor's place, as spiritual descendant of the shaman and unfrocked cousin of the priest, to examine the conflicting truths that society has found too dangerous to embrace. As Shakespeare has asked 'What should such fellows as I do crawling between heaven and earth?'[3] The greatest of life's tensions is that between life and death: Eros and Thanatos. It has been left to the actor to attempt to deal in the truly erotic – not titillating or pornographic – with Eros as the fundamentally creative and sustaining force in humankind's physical existence. To embrace this together with Thanatos and to share the mystery, the joys and fears with the audience. The very sacrificial nature of acting lies in the exploration and reconciliation of this final dichotomy: within death thou shalt find life. The tension existing between the two forces gives power and energy to the actor's task.

Performance itself takes place in the interstices between actor and text; actor, text and space; actor, text, space and audience. 'Acting resonates within the paradoxes of human action': the making of self, of sign, of meaning. In the very tension and agreement between dichotomies lies the search for truth and the revelation of the mystery: in the gap between mask and face, where the presence and absence of truth is revealed.

The idea of a truth in conflict with itself brings us, in a somewhat ironical manner, to a topic we feel obliged, in concluding, to give a nod towards: the conceit of post-modernism. The sensibility of the post-modern has been creeping up on us since well back into the nineteenth century. Basically, it reverses the position of humanism in its search for order, value structure and continuity, in order to 'privilege' multiplicity, self-reflexive irony, and mutually destabilizing collage. Rather more simply put, post-modernism and its critical underpinning of deconstruction challenges the possibility of any communicable presence of the actor that we can take as knowable. In other words, the actor/sign can never be filled with a meaning which can be universally accepted by the audience. The gap we spoke of above is not fillable because it is subject to Derrida's concept of *différance*; a neologism suggesting that there is always a time/space interval between word and referent, signifier and signified. (A not too dissimilar problem from that of the semioticians.) For Derrida there is a slippage between thought and expression – speech or writing – which prevents a fullness being present in action: that which is signified can never be in touch with original meaning. Thus no definite statements of universal truth can be made. There can be no closure, i.e. specific meaning in a text or performance.

This, together with another post-modern concept, that of socially constructed realities, has significant implications for acting. Director Jonathan Miller has said that the world is an emergent fiction, something that, like artists, we fabricate in every moment of our lives. Social structures and ethical systems may no longer be perceived as 'natural' or 'universal', but are constructed by humankind as it develops, and according to its current needs. Meaning, value, identity are all thrown into the melting pot. There are no longer any universal truths or self-evident facts; only those which are appropriate for a given time: like the American constitution (based upon the premise of self-evident facts), there has to be constant reinterpretation to accord with changing human circumstances. Reality becomes a transformable stage illusion which, as Prospero tells us in *The Tempest* (Act IV, Scene i): 'like the baseless fabric of this vision . . . shall dissolve. . . . Leave not a rack behind.' Life is an illusion opening out within illusions; what Ann Righter has called 'the infinite regression of a set of Chinese boxes'.[4] This concept of human condition was well put by Salman Rushdie in *Satanic Verses*:

O the dissociation of which the human mind is capable. . . . O the conflicting selves jostling within these bags of skin. No wonder we are unable to remain focused on anything for a very long time; no wonder we invent remote control, channel hopping devices.[5]

The idea of no fixed identity, of 'conflicting selves jostling within bags of skin', clearly runs against the received Stanislavski concept of through-line of character, and of any direct, naturalistic relationship between mask and face. The post-modern style of production tends to deconstruct the idea of a logo-centric character, leading to what Howard Barker has called: 'The permanent disruption of character . . . the instability of motive'.[6] It suggests a discontinuous form of acting based upon eclectic 'bytes' of life: the mirror which theatre holds up to nature will now have many matrices – will reflect the many possible selves of contemporary humankind, together with images that are segments of the past, in overlay and contradiction with the present.

It is here that our intuition of acting as the creation of a series of masks seems equally appropriate to serve the work of the actor in post-modern production. There will now be many masks in one performance; masks may even be worn over masks, so as to make playfully ironical comments on our very concept of the idea of a unique self or character (indeed, consciously to deconstruct the received concept of a Hamlet, or a Lear). But the actor's task will still be the creation of the appropriate mask for the moment of action; through the use of technique: process and skills. Technique will still provide the actor with a firm infrastructure for work in the apparently shifting sands of post-modern performance demands.

While technique will continue to serve the actor, there is a danger that the post-modern emphasis upon self-serving, plastic images, the playful juggling of centrifugal, highly coloured selves, will lead to an absence – in the sense of void – at the heart of acting: a Las Vegas of the soul. To avoid this, there will be a greater need for the actor to hold fast to the 'idea' of acting that has been passed down from shamanic ancestors. That need to touch the mystery and reveal it in whatever form: the constantly moving attempt to illuminate the mystery in the light of a given time.

The human condition may no longer be seen as cast in universals, but it is a continuum. The similar purpose of human myths, rituals and dramatic performance across space and time suggests an ongoing need to understand the mystery, the otherness, the absence which is made present in theatre by the undeniable fact of the actor's thereness. 'Hither coming whence; whither going hence?' is an eternal question. Answers may change, but the desire for understanding remains, and the actor continues to perform the

protean and chameleon task of reflecting and researching the different hopes and possibilities of life, in the face of the reality of
absence and death. Social and philosophical conditions may
change complexion, but the ontological task remains. Outer masks
change, but the spirit of the mask must remain to illuminate the
current aspect of the eternal condition. A desire for understanding
is the common thread. That understandings may differ at different
times, that the idea of understanding itself may be viewed ironically, does not negate the process.

Precisely because we no longer believe in magical ceremonies,
in 'efficacious rituals', we need the actor's presence to make the
absence felt. If it is an illusion, it is a necessary one. Cocteau has
said, 'as these mysteries are beyond us let us pretend we are
organizing them'. To pretend is the actor's task. There will always
be the need to create the intimation of the fullness that Derrida
and deconstruction may deny. The actor tries to keep us in touch
with that which is beyond understanding, that which 'passeth
show'. This imaginal world of our overarching humanity. We must
hope that the post-modern conception of the world as a series of
'acts', in which 'everyone will be famous for fifteen minutes', will
not kill off the spiritual function of acting, camp it out of all
context, and smother it beneath a vulgar excess of spurious role-
playing: the outer trappings of the mask rather than the spirit of
the mask itself.

Monsieur Derrida, respected critic, semanticist, polemicist, is
not, finally, an actor. Whereas deconstruction is to some extent
an intellectual game, actors physically experience the possession,
the presence that is involved in the act of acting. Mystery, otherness and absence is made present by the coincidence of face and
mask, actor and role. Playing takes place within the gap, the
interplay of mask and face. Call the gap *différance*, it remains a
notion that refers, however oppositionally, to what Hegel has called
Geist, or spirit; to the presence and movement of an ongoing human
consciousness. Nor does acting ever enforce closure. The curtain
falls, but the actors rise and move on, seeking, in whatever mask
is appropriate to the sensibility of the time, to 'try to please you
every day'. Here is no closure; here is comment and continuity.

Critical positions may come and go and have their temporal
influence upon the shape and style of performance: as Jean
Rostand has said, 'Les Théories passent. Le Grenouille reste'.[7] But

acting, as idea and effect, stems from the basic needs, hopes, joys and fears of humankind; it is likely to survive deconstruction as it survived the Romans, the Puritans and the best efforts of the semioticians. The human body as sign and (dare I say it) the human soul as spirit remain, though detail and dynamics may change. As Ecclesiastes tells us: 'That which hath been is now, and that which is to be hath already been.' Acting, through its very intangibility, will continue to try to reach and reveal the ultimate and all-embracing mystery to which all human beings – be they black, white, brown, male or female – are subject: what it means to walk between Heaven and Hell and to flirt with (be it as tragic hero, comic clown, or post-modern metaphor), though never to understand, the dynamic and dangerous presence of death within life.

David Richards, in a *New York Times* review of a post-modern production of *Henry IV, Part 1* in which Poins wore an automobile tyre around his neck and drank Budweiser beer, among other deconstructive conceits, has said, 'There is only one condition really, you have got to believe the actors.'[8] Ultimately, the potency of acting may lie in the very fact that it is beyond our ability simply to describe – lying, as it does, in some deeply rooted genetic code where hope for life, fear of death, superstition, instinct, intellect and sexuality collide. The need to act drives that potentially dangerous outsider whom we ask to bring us both *dulce* and *utile*. The paradox of whose power has kept him and her outside the bounds of polite society, seen them whipped from parish boundaries, refused burial in consecrated ground. The actor. Who must continue to have the courage, curiosity and concern to go out and 'do it in the road'; and probably frighten the horses.

Notes

INTRODUCTION

1 A. Guinness, *Blessings in Disguise*, New York, Alfred A. Knopf, 1985.
2 *Hamlet*, Act III, Scene ii.
3 W.B. Yeats, *Among School Children*, from *The Tower* collection, 1928.

1 ACTING AND THE PHENOMENOLOGICAL PROBLEM

1 D. Diderot, *Le Paradoxe sur le comédien* (1st edn 1830); *The Paradox of Acting*, trans. W.H. Pollock, New York, Hill & Wang, 1957.
2 L. Pirandello, *Six Characters in Search of an Author* (1st edn 1921), trans. F. May, London, Heinemann, 1980.
3 Bert States elaborates on this idea in *Great Reckonings in Little Rooms*, Berkeley, University of California Press, 1985, pp. 160–3.

2 ACTING AND SEMIOTICS

1 J. Hollingshead, *My Lifetime*, London, S. Low Marston & Co., 1895, pp. 189–90.
2 Martin Esslin makes this point in his *The Field of Drama*, London, Methuen, 1987, pp. 165–6.
3 B. Brecht, *Mother Courage* (1st edn 1939), trans. Eric Bentley, London, Methuen, 1962.

5 THE PSYCHOLOGY IN ACTING

1 W. Worthen, *The Idea of the Actor*, Princeton, Princeton University Press, 1984, p. 76.
2 H. Home, *Elements of Criticism*, New York, Collins, 1830, p. 195.
3 D. Diderot, *Le Paradoxe sur le comédien* (1st edn 1830); *The Paradox of Acting*, trans. W.H. Pollock, New York, Hill & Wang, 1957.
4 W. Archer, *Masks or Faces* (1st edn 1888), New York, Hill & Wang, 1957.

5 B. Matthews (ed.), *Papers on Acting*, New York, Hill & Wang, 1958, p. 26.
6 K. Stanislavski, *An Actor Prepares* (1st edn 1927), trans. E. Hapgood, New York, Theatre Arts Books, 1948.
7 K. Stanislavski, *Building a Character*, trans. E. Hapgood, New York, Theatre Arts Books, 1949.
8 K. Stanislavski, *Creating a Role*, trans. E. Hapgood, New York, Theatre Arts Book, 1961.
9 R. Lewis, *Method or Madness*, New York, Samuel French, 1958.
10 V. Redgrave, *Acting in the Sixties*, ed. H. Burton, London, BBC Publications, 1970, p. 166.
11 F. Wedekind in R. Corrigan (ed.), *The Modern Theatre*, New York, Macmillan, 1964, p. 224.
12 C. Marowitz, *The Act of Being*, London, Martin Secker & Warburg, 1978, p. 14.

6 THE DYNAMICS OF ACTING: SKILLS

1 *Hamlet*, Act II, Scene ii.
2 *Hamlet*, Act III, Scene ii.
3 ibid.

7 THE DYNAMICS OF ACTING: PROCESS

1 This return to the primacy of sign was almost a precondition for the presentational sensibility of much of the drama of the latter half of the twentieth century, paving the way for responses to the fractured existential condition of contemporary life of Brecht, Artaud and the absurdists.
2 R. Laban, *The Mastery of Movement*, London, Macdonald & Evans, 1960.
3 C. Marowitz, *The Act of Being*, London, Martin Secker & Warburg, 1978, p. 22.
4 H. Blau, *The Audience*, Baltimore, Johns Hopkins University Press, 1990, p. 178.
5 D. Sullivan, 'The mask as force behind', *Los Angeles Times*, 25 October 1981, p. 45.
6 M. St-Denis, *Theatre, The Rediscovery of Style*, London, Heinemann, 1960.
7 R. Schechner, *Environmental Theatre*, New York, Hawthorne, 1973, p. 165.
8 J. Mortimer, *Clinging to the Wreckage*, London, Weidenfeld & Nicolson, 1982, p. 72.

8 THE DYNAMICS OF ACTING: STYLE

1 M. Doran, *Endeavors of Art*, Madison, University of Wisconsin Press, 1954, p. 233.

2 J. Grotowski, *Towards a Poor Theatre*, London, Methuen, 1969, p. 209.
3 L. Page, 'Emotion is a theatrical weapon', *New Theatre Quarterly*, May 1990, p. 179.
4 The desire to be seen in a 'positive' light, to be liked, is an obstacle most young actors have to overcome. This they do as soon as they learn that it is not goodness *per se*, but wrestling with the darker side of the human persona that is the most powerfully attractive on stage.

11 THE CYBERNETICS OF ACTING: AUDIENCE AND CRITIC

1 S. Brett, *What Bloody Man is That?*, New York, Doubleday Dell, 1988.
2 ibid., pp. 195–6.
3 *Hamlet*, Act I, Scene i.
4 S. Callow, *Being an Actor*, London, Methuen, 1984, p. 164.

12 ACTING AS DANGER AND SACRIFICE

1 J.-J. Rousseau, *Politics and the Arts*, trans. A. Bloom, Glencoe Ill., Free Press, 1960, pp. 79–80.
2 Quoted in G. Playfair, *Kean: The Life and Paradox of the Great Actor*, London, Reinhardt & Evans, 1950, p. 104.
3 ibid., p. 240.
4 D. Bogarde, *Backcloth*, London, Penguin, 1987.
5 Quoted by Brian Bates, *The Way of the Actor*, Boston, Shambhala Publications Inc., 1987, p. 19.
6 *Time*, 8 August 1977, p. 14.
7 S. Callow, *Being an Actor*, London, Methuen, 1984.
8 M. Malone, *Foolscap*, New York, Little Brown and Company, 1991, p.269.
9 'J. Guare: Criticism, interview, playography', *New Theatre Quarterly*, vol. III, no. 10 (May 1987), p. 175.
10 *Hamlet*, Act II, Scene i.

CODA

1 D. Diderot, *The Paradox of Acting* (1st edn 1830), trans. W.H. Pollock, New York, Hill & Wang, 1957.
2 W. Archer, *Masks or Faces* (1st edn 1888), New York, Hill & Wang, 1957.
3 *Hamlet*, Act III, Scene i.
4 A. Righter, *Shakespeare and the Idea of the Play*, London, Penguin, 1967.
5 S. Rushdie, *Satanic Verses*, New York, Viking, 1989, p. 463.
6 H. Barker, *Guardian*, 22 August 1988, p. 34.
7 'Theories pass. The frog remains', J. Rostand, *Carnets d'un biologiste*.
8 D. Richards, *New York Times*, 10 March 1991, p. 5.

Select bibliography

A select, annotated bibliography for those who are interested in further reading in this area.

Bates, B. (1987) *The Way of the Actor*, Boston: Shambhala Publications. Certainly the best, possibly the only reliable discussion of the actor's function by a psychologist. Based upon seven years of work with students at the Royal Academy of Dramatic Art and interviews with leading actors. While of interest to the casual reader, the book is embraceable by the professional, owing to its great virtue of being written from the actor's rather than the psychologist's viewpoint.

Blau, H. (1990) *The Audience*, Baltimore: Johns Hopkins University Press. A comprehensive and erudite discussion of what constitutes the nature of an audience, and its relationship to the stage event. Not easy reading: essentially for the critic and theatre scholar.

Brett, S. (1987) *What Bloody Man is That?*, New York: Doubleday Dell. No better flavour of the life of a working, or 'resting', actor can be found than in this mystery story (one of a series) by former actor Simon Brett. Through the frequently glazed eyes of his hero, Charles Paris, Brett takes an acute, affectionate, humorously ironical look at the daily trials of a seldom-working professional. True, and eminently readable.

Callow, S. (1984) *Being An Actor*, London: Methuen. The most forthright book written by an actor upon the exigencies of a professional career. Set down with an avowed partiality, a strong flavour of the man comes through, and the controversial energy and humour of the book make it an invaluable document on the life of at least one actor in his and our time.

Goldman, M. (1975) *The Actor's Freedom*, New York: The Viking Press. A critical work of enormous scope which, while deftly dealing with the idea of phenomenological doubleness of the actor, ranges across the whole spectrum of the drama. A scholarly but readable work, crucial to the contemporary student of theatre.

Guinness, A. (1985) *Blessings in Disguise*, New York: Alfred A. Knopf.

The most urbane actor autobiography. An elegant, witty and intelligent record of a great period in British theatre. Informed throughout by the humane sensibility that underlies the best purposes of acting.

Lewis, R. (1958) *Method or Madness*, New York: Samuel French.
The 'classic' look at the evolution of the Method in the United States, by a highly insightful, original member of the Group Theater. It puts in perspective and clarifies the nature of the rift over emotion memory. Also full of pithy and amusing truths about the reality of an actor's work.

Marowitz, C. (1978) *The Act of Being*, London: Martin Secker & Warburg.
Written by the American, self-confessed charlatan, who first introduced the Method to England, and has since reneged. It has all the vehemence of new-found apostasy. It also happens to be very astute in its discussion of the different demands upon an actor made by the fissiparous nature of contemporary drama. And, with its somewhat jaundiced director's view of actors, it provides a nice balance for Simon Callow's view of directors.

Redfield, W. (1969) *Letters from an Actor*, New York: Viking Press.
Basically an account of the production of *Hamlet* in which John Gielgud directed Richard Burton; Redfield was Guildenstern. Not only a fascinating and perceptive record of a 'stellar' company in action, but a book full of wit, wisdom, passion and intelligence. Ranks with Antony Sher as the best revelation by an actor of the manic gaiety and despair of acting in full process.

Sher, A. (1985) *Year of the King*, London: Chatto & Windus.
Highly readable account of the evolution of Sher's remarkable *Richard III*. A fascinating record of an actor's physical, intellectual and emotional process in creating and playing a role. Equally it gives a strong sense of the nature of 'a life in art' in general.

States, B. (1985) *Great Reckonings in Little Rooms*, Berkeley: University of California Press.
A lucid, elegant and accessible discourse on the phenomenological problem of theatre. Deals critically with the full range of an actor's complex relationship to script, audience and stage.

Worthen, W. (1984) *The Idea of the Actor*, Princeton: Princeton University Press.
A wide-ranging discussion of the critical theories of acting from the Renaissance to the present day. Essentially for the student of theatre, it focuses upon the manner in which the ethics of drama and the ethics of acting have been interpenetrating and mutually sustaining.

Index

director, the, 10, 28, 91–9; and
    interpretation, 93, 94
Doran, Madeleine, 74
dramatis persona, 40, 71
drink and the actor, 113–14
Duse, Eleonora, 2, 8

Elizabethan theatre, 10
emotion, 34–6, 50; memory, 22, 40,
    52, 58, 69, 71
employment, 26, 29, 30
eroticism: of acting, 107, 112, 113,
    122, 126
Evans, Edith, 82

fan: use of, 89
farce, 21, 49, 50, 69, 88
Feldenkrais, Moshe, 24, 77
film acting, 84, 101
fourth wall, the, 9, 113
frame: in camera work, 86; stage
    as, 10, 11, 19, 83
Freud, Sigmund, 28, 36, 38, 74;
    Freudian slip, 53

games: as acting tool, 60–3
Garrick, David, 2, 35
'gaze': of audience, 102, 103
gesture, 10, 14, 34, 46–8, 88, 118;
    economy of, 47
Gielgud, John, 8, 63, 71, 84
given circumstances, 53, 54, 56, 71,
    77
Goethe, Johann Wolfgang Von:
    and rules for actors, 13
Greek theatre: acting in, 84, 85;
    and audience, 102
Grotowski, Jerzy, 21, 24, 66, 76, 77
ground plan, 83, 87, 88
Group Theater, The, 38
Guare, John, 120
Guinness, Alec, 1, 3, 8, 62

Hagen, Uta, 71
Hall, Peter, 44
Hill, Aaron, 34, 36
Hill, John, 34, 36
Horner, 53, 70

humours: vocabulary of, 33

'If', the, 53
imagination, 27, 55, 57, 88, 89
Importance of Being Earnest, The, 61,
    83, 122
improvization, 60–4, 76
individualism, 37, 42, 79
inner process, 36, 40, 53

Jackson, Glenda, 24, 77
Jefferson, Thomas, 38
Jung, Karl, 77

Kowalski, Stanley, 53, 70

Laban, Rudolf, 57, 59
Lewis, Robert, 42
liberalism: of the actor, 115

Macbeth, 16
Madonna, 43
Marat/Sade, the, 74, 77, 78
Marowitz, Charles, 43, 59
mask: of character, 27, 40, 73, 75,
    78–81, 85, 86, 89, 95, 111, 116,
    117, 118, 125; as training process,
    64–70
Masks or Faces, 35, 121
melodrama, 8, 13
memorization, 96, 97
Method, the, 4, 22, 35, 38–43, 53,
    59
Method or Madness, 42
Meyerhold, Vsevlod, 24, 55, 65, 77
Midsummer Night's Dream, A, 74, 104
Miller, Arthur, 38, 42
Miller, Jonathan, 122
mise-en-scène, 15, 48, 81, 87
Molière, 7, 10, 65, 66
Mortimer, John, 70
Moscow Art Theatre, The, 38
Mother Courage, 16
muscular memory, 21, 24, 58
'mystery' in acting, 92, 117, 119,
    122, 124, 125, 126